ADVA

M000307986

"Having worked with Ben over the years, I wholeheartedly recommend his approach to making purpose accessible to leaders across different sectors and organizations."
Andy Cosslett, Chairman, Kingfisher PLC

"At My Hotels, we understand that great service should always be organic and from the heart. My partnership with Ben extends over 25 years, in which he has consistently given great service to his clients inspired by his purpose. *Purpose* is a great distillation of his insight, encouraging the reader to lead from the heart."
Andreas Thrasy, Founder and Chairman, My Hotels

"Most leaders claim to value human dignity; far too many discard it quickly when under pressure at work. *Purpose* is a call to arms to reinforce humanity in the workplace and follow what matters most."
Cheryl Bachelder, author of *Dare To Serve* and former CEO, Popeyes Louisiana Kitchen Inc.

"Ben Renshaw writes about one of the most important drives in our life – our sense of purpose. In this book you'll explore all the ways purpose can guide, motivate, and fulfill you, both personally and organizationally. If you're on a search for meaning, this is the book for you."
Daniel H. Pink, author of *Drive* and *When*

"As an association, our purpose is to represent, protect and promote the interest of our global members. A key ingredient is to support our members in being able to fulfil their own purpose. We have been fortunate to partner with Ben over the years and *Purpose* represents his best work."
Don Berg, CEO, IHG Owners Association

"What can only you do? This is one of the most important questions a leader can ask. In *Purpose*, Ben challenges readers to look inside themselves to define their crucial 'why?', which will shape their answer. Having known Ben's work for over 15 years, he is one of the best coaches in the business."
Graham Alexander, Founder and Chairman, The Alexander Partnership, originator of the GROW model, author of *Tales From The Top* and co-author of *SuperCoaching*

"Following 25 years of global transaction expertise as a partner at top tier law firms, I had the opportunity to define my purpose with Ben. As a result, I co-founded Blue River Group, Australia's independent impact investment services firm. We are a profit with purpose business. Reading *Purpose* is like benefitting from personal coaching with Ben."
Grant Fuzi, Co-CEO & Founder, Blue River Group

"Companies whose success is founded on creating meaning for their employees, as well as for their customers and stakeholders, have an invigorating sense of purpose that goes beyond business success and which makes people feel they are changing society. I welcome *Purpose* as a way to create our own sense of meaning."
Gurnek Bains, Founder and CEO, Global Future CIC, author of *Meaning.Inc*

"Heathrow is on a journey to transform our passenger service inspired by our purpose, Making Every Journey Better. Ben has been a key partner developing our senior leaders and his new book *Purpose* reflects the great work we have done."
John Holland-Kaye, CEO, Heathrow

"I've always said that inspiring leadership is about getting others to believe in themselves, believe in your cause, and then achieve more than they thought was possible. Purpose is at the heart of your cause and I highly recommend *Purpose* for anyone wanting to become more inspiring."
Kevin Murray, author of *People with Purpose*

"As Australasia's authority on M&A culture integration, I recognize that purpose has a critical impact on how to bring organizations together in a positive way. Ben's book on *Purpose* is a proven methodology to integrate purpose for successful outcomes."
Linley Watson, author of *Avoiding The M&A Failure Club*

"Bringing together the best business brains from Henley Business School and our network, we generate challenging thinking and constructive debate between senior leaders from many organizations and sectors. Ben's contribution through *Purpose* has stretched senior leaders to accelerate their growth."
Mark Swain, Director, The Henley Partnership, Henley Business School

"As a critical component of an aviation industry that keeps people and nations connected, business flowing and economies growing, NATS purpose is 'Advancing aviation, keeping the skies safe'. In *Purpose,* Ben makes an important call to action about the power of purpose to advance your future."
Martin Rolfe, CEO, NATS

"My mission is simple. I want to help successful people achieve positive, lasting change in behaviour; for themselves, their people and their teams. *Purpose* is a great contribution to helping make lives better and everyone should read it."
Marshall Goldsmith, author of *What Got You Here Won't Get You There*, and corporate America's pre-eminent Executive Coach

"Teaching people how to be brilliant is my life's purpose. Finding your purpose, using it to improve your life and the lives of others should be one of the most important missions of your life. *Purpose* will show you how."
Michael Heppell, best-selling author of *How to Be Brilliant*

"Having fulfilled my dream to offer the best and widest range of organic foods available, while bringing a sense of discovery and adventure into food shopping, I encourage everyone to read *Purpose* and discover their sense of purpose and adventure for life."
Renée Elliott, Founder, Planet Organic

"In my time as CFO, CEO and now as a non-executive director, I have seen many times, at first hand, that for a company to perform at its best, leaders need to perform at their best. This requires a range of conditions to be in place such as having a clear ambition, success measures and a strategic plan. However, one fundamental requirement stands out – a unifying purpose that points everyone in the right direction. *Purpose* will point you in the right direction."
Richard Solomons, ex-CEO, IHG® PLC

"Aman destinations are renowned for space and privacy. We seek out transformative experiences for our guests. *Purpose* will take you on a transformative experience designed to help you discover what you want to be renowned for."
Roland Fasel, Chief Operating Officer, Aman

"The way to get the best out of people is to help them to discover and live their purpose. Putting this at the heart of their work enables them to deliver outstanding performance for an organization and ensures they keep growing and loving what they do. Having worked with Ben over 20 years in a range of industries including aviation, retail and telecommunications, *Purpose* is a true representation of his best thinking."
Siân Evans, Head of Talent & Development, Sainsbury's

"As an entrepreneur, the way to grow is to dare mighty things. Following your purpose gives you the courage to dare. Ben has been a constant support over the last 20 years as Yo! has grown and reading *Purpose* will challenge you to find your big dare."
Simon Woodroffe, Founder, Yo! Sushi

"Our purpose is to make a difference to people's lives. We do this by focusing on one coffee, one customer and one store at a time – always trying to be the best at what we do. *Purpose* is a great reminder to stay focused on the difference you want to make in people's lives and being the best you can be."
Will Stratton-Morris, UK CEO, Caffe Nero

"Britvic's purpose is to make life's everyday moments more enjoyable. I am a firm believer in the power of purpose to provide the necessary focus in a disruptive world to ensure that we stay on track to enjoy and be fulfilled in our work and lives."
Zareena Brown, HR Director, Britvic

Published by
LID Publishing Limited
The Record Hall, Studio 204,
16-16a Baldwins Gardens,
London EC1N 7RJ, UK

524 Broadway, 11th Floor, Suite 08-120,
New York, NY 10012, US

info@lidpublishing.com
www.lidpublishing.com

A member of:

BPR
Business Publishers Roundtable

www.businesspublishersroundtable.com

© Ben Renshaw, 2018
© LID Publishing Limited, 2018

Printed in Great Britain by TJ International
ISBN: 978-1-911498-83-4

Cover and page design: Caroline Li & Matthew Renaudin
Photography: Cambridge Jones & Eg White

PURPOSE

The extraordinary benefits of
focusing on what matters most

Ben Renshaw

LONDON   MONTERREY
MADRID   SHANGHAI
MEXICO CITY BOGOTA
NEW YORK   BUENOS AIRES
BARCELONA SAN FRANCISCO

What is your purpose? This is probably the single most important question you can ask and your answer will shape your future. However, it's not straightforward. We are led to believe that our purpose is connected with how much we achieve, the accumulation of possessions or attaining status in society. Nothing could be further from the truth.

Your personal purpose is your internal compass. It is your big why. It is the meeting point between your passion and your talent. When you are on purpose you are in flow. When you are on purpose you unlock the necessary skillset to thrive in today's complex and unpredictable world. Ultimately your personal purpose is an aspirational reason for being. A deep conviction about what is most important. It shapes your mindset, behaviour and actions. It has a timeless quality, which is beyond circumstance. It provides the meaning and direction of your life.

Purpose is your handbook for discovering and leading with purpose.

CONTENTS

PREFACE

At InterContinental Hotels Group PLC (IHG®), our purpose is to provide True Hospitality for everyone. It's a commitment that runs through all our brands and unites our people behind a common aim. As CEO, it is a privilege to lead a purpose-led organization, and to see how powerfully this can contribute to a business's long-term success. It helps define our culture and engage our teams, whether they are working with guests, third-party hotel owners, partners or in the communities in which we operate.

Having a clear purpose is equally important on an individual level. Having worked closely with Ben over the years, he has played an important role in developing many of our senior leaders to lead with purpose.

Purpose is for people wanting to reach new levels of meaning, performance and to accelerate growth.

Keith Barr, Chief Executive Officer, IHG®

INTRODUCTION

I was brought up to perform. As a classical violinist trained at the world-renowned Yehudi Menuhin School, a specialist music school nestled in the rich beauty of the English countryside, I woke up religiously every morning at 6am to start practising before breakfast from the age of 8 years old. This went on for the next 12 years as I toured the world giving concerts in places as diverse as China, India, America and across Europe. Although I was talented and at the top of my game, there was something missing. I was not happy and did not want to pursue a musical career.

This realization came to a head when I started a four-year performer's course at The Guildhall School of Music and Drama and, within weeks, I knew that the music profession was not for me. I found that I didn't have the sufficient passion to make music my life. I wasn't inspired enough to dedicate all my time and energy to being the best violinist I could be. I came to realize that what was missing was a clear and compelling purpose about why I was doing what I was doing and what it meant to me.

As a result, I was in torment. I knew I faced losing the years I had invested in becoming a great violinist but, at the same time, I was at peace. Although I didn't know what was around the corner, I knew that the first step was to stop doing what wasn't working. I then embarked on a personal journey of self-discovery to clarify what I really wanted to do, what I truly loved, what I was passionate about and why I was doing what I was doing. After considerable soul searching it came down to one thing. People. The aspect I did enjoy about music was all about people. I loved playing with other musicians and interacting with an audience. I realized that my interest in life was relationships and learning about the complexity of human relations.

My fascination in relationships led me to consider training as a psychologist; however as I was preparing to study psychology at university, I was introduced to the world of personal development by my aunt, who had attended courses in self-discovery. I embarked on a journey where I specialized in areas such as relationships, happiness, success and coaching where I finally landed in the world of leadership.

In 2007, I was invited to co-design and deliver the Senior Leadership Development Programme for InterContinental Hotels Group PLC (IHG®). IHG® is one of the world's leading hotel companies with more than 350,000 people working across almost 100 countries. Their organizational purpose is to deliver 'Great Hotels Guests Love®'. Sponsored by Andy Cosslett, a former CEO, and co-designed with their former HR Director Tracy Robbins, we created their senior leadership programme entitled 'Leading with Purpose'. Over the next 10 years I had the privilege of developing more than 1,000 of their top leaders in Asia, the Middle-East, India, Australasia, America and Europe which has crystallized some important lessons about purpose:

LESSONS ON PURPOSE

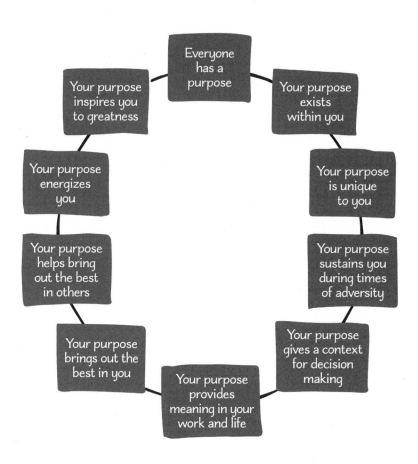

Everyone has a purpose

Your purpose exists within you

Your purpose is unique to you

Your purpose sustains you during times of adversity

Your purpose gives a context for decision making

Your purpose provides meaning in your work and life

Your purpose brings out the best in you

Your purpose helps bring out the best in others

Your purpose energizes you

Your purpose inspires you to greatness

Since building my purpose credentials with IHG®, I have had the opportunity to enable other big organizations in a range of sectors including aviation, banking, FMCG, law, manufacturing, retail and technology to lead with purpose, as well as scores of individual leaders and teams. My experience has led to the realization and conviction that unless people and organizations discover and live their purpose, the opportunity to fulfil their potential is limited. Purpose is the catalyst for personal meaning. Purpose is the glue that binds teams together. Purpose is the inspiration that enables organizations to outperform.

In terms of linking purpose and leadership, my belief is that everyone is a leader, whether someone has a formal role in an organization, or by taking a lead in their own life. The vital question everyone needs to ask is who are they? I have found this question to be one of the most confronting to answer. As Socrates wisely said, *"People make themselves appear ridiculous when they are trying to know obscure things before they know themselves."* Through a passionate inquiry of existence and identity, Socrates put 'Know Thyself' at the core of his philosophy.

A purpose helps you to know who you really are as it is the essence of your real self. Clarifying and following your own purpose is the most fundamental ingredient required to understanding the 'why', 'what' and 'how' of your life and making sense of the complexity of your existence.

This book is the distillation of my key learnings about how to lead with purpose. By applying the insight contained in the following chapters your leadership and life will improve for the better.

Ben Renshaw, London 2018

CHAPTER 1

THE
CASE FOR
PURPOSE

WHY PURPOSE?

Purpose is an aspirational reason for being which inspires and provides a call to action

Your personal purpose is your raison d'être – your reason for being. It is what gives your life meaning, direction and inspiration. It is a deep sense of knowing what is true for you which, if you follow, will ensure that you flourish, be the best version of yourself and fulfil your potential. I believe that probably the most significant part of your life's journey is to discover what your purpose is. Your life's joy is to live it.

To discover your purpose requires an open mind and a genuine willingness focused on peak experiences in your life. When you are on purpose you are at your best. When you are on purpose you are in flow. When you are on purpose you are inspired. The act of reflecting upon lifetime highlights and defining what they mean to you will bring together the key themes that are most precious to you such as making a difference, adding value and creating possibility. By continuing to dig deeper into why these are so important to you, you will learn the essence of your big 'why', which is at the heart of your purpose.

We live in disruptive times. Deadly terrorist attacks. Extreme weather. Large scale migration. Cyber security. Economic inequality. Societal polarization. Fake news ... I could go on and on. So how should we stay sane in turbulent times? What path should we follow? Who should we believe? What actions should we take?

The starting point for relating to the world today is through the lens of purpose. As Mark Zuckerberg wisely stated in his commencement address at Harvard University, *"In our generation, the struggle of whether we connect more, whether we achieve our biggest opportunities, comes down to this – your ability to build communities and create a world where every single person has a sense of purpose."*

The time for purpose is now. Finding your purpose and learning to apply it from a range of perspectives including personal, leadership, team, organizational and societal is critical to navigate the uncertainty of our world.

It was the winter before the turn of the millennium and I was in New Zealand, the homeland of my wife Veronica. We were at Piha, our favourite beach, famous for its big surf on the west coast of the North Island, 40 km from Auckland. We had been married for a couple of years and as we walked down the beach Veronica turned to me and said that she wanted to start a family. My immediate response was to say, *"I'm too busy."* This did not go down so well and she gently informed me that she was going to start a family with or without me! It was a time for soul searching.

Upon reflection, I realized that one of my main reasons for not wanting to have children was a family joke that my father didn't want to have kids. He was passionate about his world of education and at the time that my sister and I were born he was immersed in his PhD and establishing his career as a university professor. I had internalized this reality and had come to believe that if you were successful in your career, why would you want children? Didn't they just get in the way of achieving your ambitions?

Once back in London I called and arranged to meet my dad for dinner. We sat down in a local restaurant and

I confided in him about my dilemma to have children and that I wanted to understand his point of view. It surprised me when he went on to say that having children was the best thing he had done, and that although he was extremely busy with his work, family came first.

I describe my personal purpose as being *'an enabler of truth'*. I have always been a seeker. I have always wanted to know what is real and what is true. I have always asked the question 'why'. Understanding my dad's view on children helped me to dig deeper about my own truth for starting a family. I realized that in fact it was my truth to try for a family and 17 years later with three amazing children I couldn't imagine it any other way. If I hadn't followed my purpose it would have been a different story.

I have identified the following seven significant benefits of leading a life with purpose:

PURPOSE BENEFITS

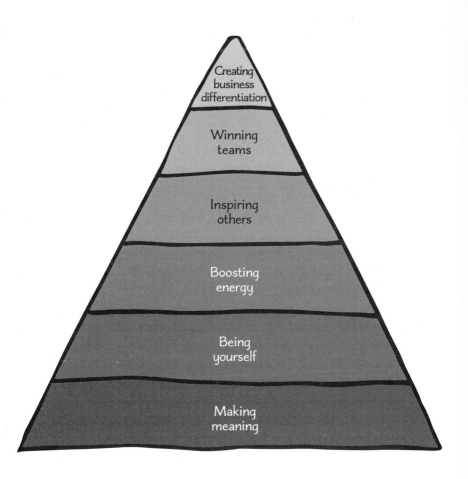

Each of these seven benefits will be explored in the remainder of this chapter.

MAKING
MEANING

Meaning provides the reason to evolve,
overcome obstacles and fulfil potential

What is the point to your work, life, relationships, leadership? A big question that requires a big answer. My experience shows that once you are clear on your purpose, you will be clear about the meaning of every aspect of your world. A purpose is your big 'why' and provides meaning about why you do what you do, why you make the choices you make and why you appreciate what you have.

From the outside Susan had it all. A strong marriage of 25 years, a mother of three wonderful children, a CEO within a thriving industry and yet was not fulfilled. She was questioning why she was so driven to be 'wonder woman' at the expense of her wellbeing. She was on the verge of quitting her role when I received her call. My advice to Susan (as is usually the case) was to focus on making any internal changes, before making any external changes. As we surveyed her landscape, what became increasingly clear is that from an early age she had taken the path of least resistance and had followed in the footsteps of the person she admired the most – her father. The result was to build up a grand life, but at the expense of her true self. Upon further inquiry, what transpired at the heart of her conflict was a lack of meaning about why she was doing what she was doing. The result was that Susan needed to discover her purpose, she needed to find what was most important to her before anything else.

My interest in purpose led me to the teachings of Victor Frankl, a prominent Viennese psychiatrist who survived World War II. His work has provided me with the most profound learning I have encountered about the need for meaning. He endured the harrowing experience of going through seven concentration camps, including Auschwitz. Due to his professional training, he was able to observe the way that both he and others in Auschwitz coped (or didn't) with the experience. He noticed that it was the men who comforted others and who gave away their last piece of bread who survived the longest. They offered him proof that everything can be taken away from us except the ability to choose our attitude in any given set of circumstances. He identified that the type of person the prisoners became was the result of an inner decision, and not influences from the camp alone. Frankl came to believe man's deepest desire is to search for meaning and purpose.

Meaning and purpose are intrinsically linked. Meaning is defined as a thing one intends to convey and the implication of a special significance. In the absence of meaning we doubt, we have uncertainty, we are unsure and we fail to understand why. By having meaning, we are clear, we have conviction, we know what is right and we have a strong why. A significant conclusion German philosopher and cultural critic Friedrich Nietzsche drew from his work, which challenged psychological diagnoses, was, *"He who has a why to live can bear almost any how."*

As I write this, we have just experienced some of the most torrid times in recent history. I believe that the way to survive these human tragedies is to somehow make sense of them so that a resolution can be reached. People will do this in their own way and in their own time. Although these atrocities are out of our hands, what does lie within our grasp is the ability to make meaning of what happens to us.

Back to Susan. Together in her coaching programme we explored her purpose. What transpired was the importance of *"inspiring others to greatness"*. I encouraged Susan to start living and leading with this on a daily basis and to see what would happen. As a mother, it gave her a new reference point to connect with her children. Rather than seeing herself as the taxi driver and disciplinarian to get things done, by focusing on inspiring them to greatness enabled her to be there for them in a different way. She became more curious, wanting to truly understand their hopes and fears. She developed more patience, listened deeply and felt a level of connection that was previously missing. As a leader, she broadened her focus from hitting targets, to creating a great place to work where everyone had the opportunity to do meaningful work and grow. Susan's purpose triggered her desire to help others and she became committed to mentoring those who were aspiring to build great careers and lives.

By focusing on creating a meaningful life, Susan recognized that her purpose lay within her. By making sense of her work, life and relationships, Susan gained new levels of fulfilment and success.

HAVING CLEAR
IDENTITY

Knowing who you are is the real knowledge to acquire

I have always found it intriguing to consider the amount of time, energy and effort we dedicate to the accumulation of knowledge, skills and experience. Yet, we tend to invest little time and effort into understanding who we really are. For instance, watching my children grow up (as I write, my daughter is 16, and my two sons are 12 and 8) I see them struggling with their own sense of identity, as they try to learn how to manage the impact of strong influencing factors such as society, culture and education. Being an educationalist at heart, I struggle with their schooling the most. Hour upon hour spent on learning facts and figures. I fully appreciate the value of developing cognitive capability, learning how to learn and improving problem solving skills; however, given that knowledge is now available to us with a simple click, surely we need to shift the emphasis from filling ourselves up with facts, to learning how we apply knowledge in a meaningful way, which in turn will impact how you see yourself.

I recently launched a new leadership development programme for a major client entitled, *'Leading Sustainable Growth'*. The programme is sponsored by the Director of People who believes that at the heart of sustainable growth is the requirement for everyone to be able to come to work as themselves and belong.

Additionally, to help senior leaders better understand their identity, the company invited a speaker, Vicky Beeching, to share her story. Vicky is a writer, broadcaster and keynote speaker with a fascinating life story. She was a well-known Christian singer/songwriter in the American 'Bible Belt' for much of her twenties, then came out as gay in 2014 at the age of 35. This shocked the church on both sides of the Pond. Her catalyst for taking this step was an aggressive auto-immune illness; her cells were literally attacking themselves, which felt to her like a physical expression of the internal battle she experienced between her faith and her sexuality.

Coming out cost Vicky her career in church music. Fuelled by her experiences, she now works in corporate diversity and inclusion, championing equality in the workplace. Sharing her story in keynote speeches, or developing people through one-to-one coaching, has become a large part of her work portfolio. She's also a champion of greater openness about mental health at work, speaking vulnerably about her own journey with depression and anxiety, and that many people can still have a successful career despite these struggles. Her message on identity is clear: *"Being yourself at work is a win-win for everyone; on an individual level people are happier and healthier, and at a company level, productivity and staff-retention increase."*

Understanding your purpose is a vital ingredient for identity. Knowing who you are, what you stand for and what makes you unique are all linked to an individual's purpose. As part of my identity, one of the things that matters most to me is wisdom. I treasure wisdom in others and admire how people go about developing their wisdom. Being known as a wise person inspires me to be the best that I can be. However, I don't believe that you can claim to be wise, it needs to be recognized by others.

At the end of a busy year, I was invited by a client to attend their end of year celebration. The evening had a medieval theme and was held in a spectacular hall decorated accordingly. As we approached our dinner tables I could see everyone had a nameplate for the seating plan. Mine was entitled, *'Sir Fount of Knowledge'*. This had a profound impact on me. To be perceived as wise by a client that I held in high regard was a sign of true success and was evidence that my identity was acknowledged by others.

I bring you back to the question, who are you? As you think about the answer, try to determine what your real identity is. Only you can decide, and your answer will inspire the outcomes in your life.

BEING YOURSELF

*When you are on purpose you are being more of
who you really are*

Today, the single most admired quality in leaders is authenticity. As recently declared by the Harvard Business Review, *"Authenticity has emerged as the gold standard for leadership."* When you distil authenticity down to its essence it means, 'to be yourself'. However, the challenge here is that in order to be yourself, you have to know yourself – this is central to your purpose. If you don't know your purpose, you cannot be yourself because you don't know the truth about yourself.

There are five key components of authenticity which when mastered will enable you to be yourself with greater skill:

AUTHENTIC MODEL

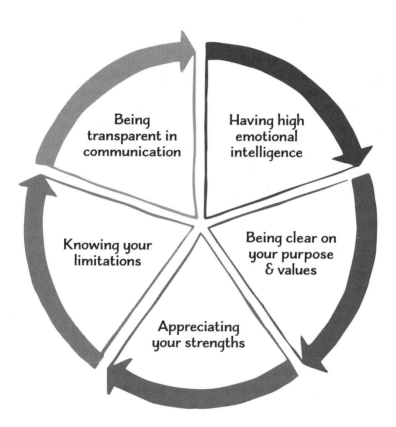

1. Having high emotional intelligence

The term 'emotional intelligence' (EQ) first appeared in a paper by Michael Beldoch in 1964, and was popularized by Daniel Goleman when he published a book with the same title in 1995. Emotional intelligence is based on four component parts: 1) Self-awareness; 2) Self-management; 3) Social awareness; 4) Social skills.

John was on a trajectory to take a senior leadership role for a major company. He had an array of impressive skills, which made him suitable for the position with a wealth of experience in commercial, operations, brands and finance. I was asked by the HR Director of the organization where John worked to conduct a feedback process. This additional data would be used by the Board to make a decision about his progression. What became apparent from my conversation with numerous stakeholders was that although people had great respect for John's technical capabilities, his main downfall was his lack of authenticity. People didn't know who he was. They couldn't get past the façade that appeared each day.

When I shared the feedback findings with John he was shocked. He didn't recognize the person being portrayed and strongly defended his position with claims that it wasn't his fault if people didn't know him and that they should learn how to read him better. As a coach, I'm used to dealing with strong reactions to feedback and so I suggested that he take some time to reflect on the data and to discuss it with his family at home. The next morning, I got an early message from John saying that he had sat down with his family over dinner and asked for their opinion about his authenticity. It was a big wake up call for him to discover that they validated the feedback findings with their own experience.

In particular there was a poignant comment made by his 15-year-old daughter who said, *"Dad, I know you love me, however you don't show it. I can't remember the last time you told me you love me and simply spent some quiet time with me listening to my thoughts and feelings."*

John was unaware of this perception, which is one of the first indicators of a lack of self-awareness – the ability to accurately assess your personal impact. He realized that he had low self-management, since his permanent busyness had stopped him from spending precious time with the most important aspect of his life, his family. His daughter's comment also drove home the fact that he was not as empathetic as he had originally thought. His inability to connect with her on an emotional level was a real gap. Finally, John realized that his social skills could do with some improvement as he was not communicating in a way that engaged others in the way he wanted.

Through processes like feedback, many leaders will realize that although they may have a high IQ, their EQ is lacking. With a low EQ, you will not have sufficient self-awareness to know whether you are being yourself or not, and how you come across in your relationships.

It is impossible to have high self-awareness, manage yourself well, deeply connect and communicate clearly with others unless you have conviction about your fundamental motivations.

2. Being clear on your purpose and values

We will be doing a deep dive on your purpose and values in the forthcoming chapters, therefore I won't cover it here; suffice to say that in order to be your authentic self you need to know and live your purpose and values.

3. Appreciating your strengths

Your strengths are your natural talent and skills, or what the author René Carayol calls 'SPIKE' (Strengths Positively Identified Kick-start Excellence) in his book of the same title. Your strengths are what you are best at; for instance, being creative, influencing, advising, connecting or organizing. When you are playing to your strengths you are being authentic, characterized by an experience of being in the zone, in flow and energized. I like the insight from Tom Rath, author of *Strengths Finder 2.0*, one of the seminal books on playing to strengths, who makes the linkage between strengths and authenticity by stating, *"Be more of who you already are."*

4. Knowing your limitations

The flip side of your strengths are your limitations. I once coached the top sales person in a company. Paul had an amazing ability to connect with people, understand their needs and deliver over and above the call of duty. Serving people was his passion and he excelled delivering the best numbers in the organization month after month. However, he suffered two sleepless nights every month when he had to run through the finances with his boss. We looked at what was going on and why this was happening. What emerged was Paul's biggest fear – to appear stupid.

When we dug around for the source of this fear, Paul remembered at school one 'supportive' teacher calling him stupid and it had stuck. We took a couple of practical steps to remedy the situation. Firstly, I encouraged Paul to take an IQ test. He had managed to miraculously avoid many of the psychometric tests that executives normally complete, but he needed to face his worst fear of having a low IQ. He went online, took a test and the results came back as above average. The next step was to get feedback from his line manager about their monthly meeting to assess the reality of the situation. Paul's manager had been aware that occasionally Paul came across as nervous and he'd wondered why, given his consistent level of performance. Paul shared his fear of coming across as stupid with him and this enabled them to work together more closely on the presentation so that Paul could sleep better.

It's important to know your limitations, but not to spend your life worrying about or trying to fix them. You will only gain marginal improvement and it will drain you along the way. The key, particularly for leaders, is to surround yourself with others who complement your skillset so that you can play to their strengths and not get derailed by your weaknesses.

5. **Being transparent in communication**

Being transparent when communicating displays evidence of your authenticity. Having been promoted to the top job in her firm, Jane was about to give her first address to her senior team. With a background in finance and an ability to be tough on the numbers, the expectation from her team was that they were going to get a grilling about performance. I sat down with Jane to explore what outcomes she wanted from this important moment. I was surprised when she said 'inspiration'. She wanted the team to feel inspired by her appointment and energized about the future. I asked her about her ideas for her presentation. Sure enough, she wanted to run through the financials! But no, that wouldn't create her desired outcome, so I challenged her to think about what would. I asked Jane to reflect on who had inspired her during her career and why. She recalled several leaders she had worked for, all of whom shared one thing in common: open and honest communication. They had an ability to connect with people through displaying appropriate vulnerability, humility and humour. Qualities that develop trust.

With that in mind Jane focused on creating a narrative designed to bring the team into her world. She shared what had shaped her leadership journey. Her father had been in the military; therefore, her family had moved every 12-24 months. By the age of 18 Jane had lived in 14 different locations and had attended 8 different schools. As a consequence, she had learned to become independent to ensure that she could keep up with the changes. However, this meant that she could come across as aloof and distant. In fact, when people got to know Jane they discovered that she was an intensely loyal friend, but there were not many people who were able to get close. Jane started working at the age of 16 as a waitress. She had pretty much worked every day since. She loved the freedom that work brought, but had developed a relentless work ethic that most other people couldn't emulate. Following the birth of her first child, Jane suffered postnatal depression. She had never told anyone at work before; however, the company was running a campaign on mental health and she wanted to be a role model for showing that you can experience mental health challenges and succeed. The feedback from the team was universal in their appreciation of Jane's authenticity. They had not expected her to be so open and greatly valued her willingness to go out on a limb. Trust was built and a foundation of openness was established from that first presentation which set the team up for success.

To be authentic requires your willingness to be vulnerable and risk being yourself. As the authors Rob Goffee and Gareth Jones write in their *Harvard Business Review* article, 'Why Should Anyone Be Led By You', in the final analysis, *"Be yourself with more skill."*

GETTING
CONNECTED

In the sharing economy, the best way
to connect is through purpose

A purpose builds relationship. It becomes the glue binding people and communities together and from a leadership perspective, leadership is relationship. No relationship, no followership. However, when you assess many leaders on their relationship skills it is surprisingly low.

I had been asked to support a company to develop their senior leaders. The company was niche in its market and owned a very bespoke space in the service industry. Founded by a visionary entrepreneur, they had enjoyed fast growth but had reached a stage where the only way to succeed going forward was to strengthen their talent pipeline. The starting point was to understand the quality of leaders already leading the business. The company used a talent assessment tool to provide an objective view, which measured leaders on a range of factors including communication, persuasion, flexibility and the development of others. As the HR Director sat me down to share the results, I could tell something was up. It transpired that the majority of leaders scored lowest on their relationship skills. They had high IQs and a drive for results, but at the expense of their ability to connect. This meant that the company had a particular challenge to boost their growth in a competitive service sector.

This is not uncommon. Most organizations where I spend time struggle with a variety of engagement factors including the provision of visible leadership, transparency of communication, diversity and inclusion. These themes have their roots in a lack of connectivity. It is a challenging dilemma because companies are primarily measured on what they deliver, not on how they do it; but at the end of the day it is people who deliver, and a key component of successful delivery is through the strength of connections built.

Once you have a clearly defined purpose you approach relationships from a different perspective. Rather than viewing others as a mechanism for getting stuff done, your purpose leads you to want to engage in a meaningful way. Daniel was one of the most results oriented and pacesetting leaders I had encountered. A chief marketing officer (CMO), he was renowned for driving deals and operating in a very transactional way. As a result of his success Daniel's company asked him to move to the Middle East and head up one of their growth regions based in Dubai. Daniel accepted but, due to his pacesetting style, he had not given sufficient consideration to the implications of doing business in a different culture.

Personal relationships and mutual trust are key to doing business in the Middle East. Daniel found this very disconcerting. The extent of his relationship building skills previously rarely extended beyond a superficial hello! Also with his team, many of whom were locals, he had hit the ground running and had been driving them hard without having stopped long enough to build a relationship.

I was asked to support Daniel and his team. In my initial diagnostic findings from the team, it became very apparent that trust was low and Daniel was missing the mark by putting task before relationships. He took the feedback well and decided that he was going to prioritize building connections with his team, followed by his clients. I encouraged Daniel to speak openly with his team, expressing his vulnerability about moving to a new culture, failing to acclimatize to the culture and recognizing where he had missed the mark. The team greatly appreciated his openness and Daniel committed to scheduling regular 1:1's with his team focused on their personal and career aspirations, not just their normal business updates. Team engagement swung right up and Daniel discovered that building connections was directly in line with his purpose, which he described as, *"Creating better outcomes for a better world."*

The great thing with purpose is that it builds relationships. It becomes the glue that binds people and communities together. I have yet to meet someone who upon discovering their purpose wanted to exclude others. I have yet to come across an organization that has formulated a core purpose but kept it in the cupboard so nobody knows what it is. A purpose unites. A purpose makes linkages. A purpose connects.

BOOSTING
ENERGY

Energy is infectious

What energizes you? What de-energizes you? Several years ago, I found myself responding to anyone who asked me how I was feeling with the answer, *"Knackered!"* This was not a response I was proud of and it was a serious red flag for how I was living. My wife and I had three young children (and we were happy to keep it that way); I found myself travelling a lot with exciting global work and writing books. All of this meant that I didn't know how to increase my energy for the better. I decided to start by looking at the sources of my energy. What transpired were several main factors including physical exercise, relationships, learning, as well as having a clear sense of purpose. I decided to address each element to ensure that I could nurture and sustain my energy.

I have always enjoyed exercise. I noticed that on the days I exercised I had more energy, but I didn't do it every day. I would come up with excuses like I'm too tired, it's too dark, cold or I haven't got the time. Then, I made the decision to exercise every day. It became a non-negotiable part of my daily activities. I have been doing it ever since and it's been a game changer. I don't push it, but when I'm home it's a jog with our dog, or when I'm travelling it's the gym, and when

I can I indulge in my favourite pastime of playing tennis. The outcome is that I'm fitter now than I was several years ago, as well as having more energy.

The next step was to look at my relationships and identify those people who energized me, and those who didn't. I made a decision – to move away from relationships that drained me. I'm not a quitter. I will work at anything until there is a solution. But I realized in some relationships it was the right thing to move on. Alongside this I decided to seek out those people who did energize me and made sure that I was deliberately spending more time with them.

Unfortunately, my formal education switched me off from a love of learning. It was only when I entered the world of personal development that my appetite for continuous learning spiked. It is now insatiable. A day without learning is a wasted day. This is true whether applied as a partner, parent, leader, manager, professional or any other role in life.

A powerful example of lifelong learning is exemplified in the mastery of the tennis player, Roger Federer. For me Federer's style of play, great conduct on the tour, being a father of four children and his successful battle against age to reclaim his Wimbledon throne is underpinned by his extraordinary drive to learn how to be the best player he can be. He is a powerful example of how when you are on purpose, playing to your strengths and putting in countless hours of practice, your energy flows.

To explore your energy, you need to consider four key capacities:

1. **Physical**
   What are your habits that nourish your physical energy? How well do you eat? How restful is your sleep? How effective are your fitness rituals? Sustaining your physical

energy requires you to make specific commitments that bring out the best in you.

2. Emotional

What are you passionate about? What do you love? What is your joy? Research from psychoneuroimmunology shows that emotions impact our health and energy. In 1985, neuropharmacologist Candace Pert, from Georgetown University, revealed that neuropeptide-specific receptors are present on the cell walls of the brain and the immune system. The discovery that neuropeptides and neurotransmitters act directly on the immune system shows their close association with emotions. Therefore, positive emotions such as passion, love and joy can boost the immune system and support your energy, whereas negative emotions like anger, anxiety, fear and depression deplete your immunity over time.

3. Intellectual

How well do you focus? How do you actively learn? How often do you practise mindfulness? There is an exciting and expanding world in neuroscience which explores how the brain works. Evidence shows that the brain has plasticity, which means that it can continue to increase intelligence through making new neural pathways. You can improve the way you focus, learn and pay attention which will, in turn, improve your intellectual firepower.

4. Spiritual

What is your purpose? What are your values? What inspires you? Focusing on these vital aspects of yourself will nourish your spiritual energy and lift you up above your normal everyday set of challenges.

As a leader one of your fundamental responsibilities is to energize others, as opposed to being an energy vampire and sucking the life out of others! Hence, to be on top of your game, it is critical to manage your physical, emotional, intellectual and spiritual capacities well.

INSPIRING
OTHERS

Being inspired, inspires others

The most important role as a leader is to inspire others. At the same time, the biggest challenge for a leader is to inspire others. Why? Because in order to inspire others, you need to be inspired yourself. You might have moments of being inspired, but how do you stay inspired on a consistent basis? This is where purpose steps in. Being connected with your purpose will inspire you. It will lift you up. It will enable you to stay focused when you are faced with obstacles, road blocks and interferences that can take you off track.

Mo was leading a Sales & Marketing function during the last recession from 2008. The slowdown affected all sectors of the economy and it was compounded by the fear of a double dip. Being in the retail sector meant that Mo faced real challenges to ensure people kept their jobs. Mo defines her purpose as, *"Creating opportunities."* As a result, she sees every setback as a set up for greater opportunity which gives her the resilience to keep going in the face of daily adversity.

Back in the dark days of the recession Mo had to keep her purpose at the forefront of all decision making. She brought her leadership team together, declared her purpose and asked them to hold her accountable to creating opportunity. She knew that at times of uncertainty it was critical to provide visible leadership, to listen to people and to communicate relentlessly. Seeing her role through a lens of opportunity motivated Mo to invest countless hours in walking the floors, connecting with colleagues and sharing a consistent story of hope. The feedback she received warmed her heart. People appreciated her transparency and commitment to finding answers. As a consequence, colleagues volunteered to be flexible in their working patterns through solutions like reducing hours and job sharing, which meant that no one was forced to lose their job and remarkably, during this difficult time, engagement scores in the company went up. By following her purpose in times of adversity, Mo stayed inspired and inspired others. This was noted by her CEO who quickly promoted her on the back of her success helping to navigate the company through turbulent times.

A survey of nearly 2,000 managers by the Chartered Management Institute and the think tank Demos revealed an inspirational gap in the leaders of UK organizations. The results showed that the single most important factor that the majority of those surveyed (55%) would like to see in their leaders was 'the ability to inspire'. From those who were surveyed, 11% revealed that they actually saw the 'ability to inspire' in their leaders.

The findings of this survey highlighted six essential elements of inspirational leadership:

1. Genuine care for people;
2. Involving everybody;
3. Showing appreciation;
4. Ensuring work is fun;
5. Showing real trust;
6. Listening to colleagues.

Think for a moment about how well you demonstrate these six attributes on a regular basis? On one occasion, I was supporting an organization to improve the quality of its leadership with a particular focus on inspiration. Following the completion of a very successful two-day conference, where we brought to life the refreshed company purpose, values and leadership framework, everyone returned to work with a renewed spring in their step. Nearly everyone! One senior leader did not buy into these types of behaviours and in a roundabout way tried to undermine the credibility of a colleague. This individual might have got away with it in the past; however, by practising the six elements of inspirational leadership, people quickly rallied against the attempted sabotage and squashed the behaviour.

The results of a highly engaged workforce, as cited by David MacLeod and Nita Clarke in their report *Engage for Success: Enhancing performance through employee engagement*, include:

- 8% greater productivity;
- 16% greater profit margin;
- 19% greater operating income;
- 2.6 times Earnings per Share (EPS) growth;
- 12% greater customer advocacy;
- 50% fewer sick days;
- 87% less likely to leave the organization.

If these outcomes are attributable to how inspiring you are as a leader, then surely it is worth developing your ability to inspire. This does not mean that you suddenly have to become a great orator or transform into a hugely charismatic personality. However, it will mean that you need to become purpose-led to enable you to lift up others.

WINNING
TEAMS

Being part of a great team makes
almost anything possible

The key foundation for a high performing team is to have a clear sense of direction. At the heart of direction sits a compelling purpose. A purpose is why the team exists. It is their North Star. Having a strong sense of purpose helps a team become joined up and travel in the same direction while they are being pulled from pillar to post with the daily demands of achieving targets, serving customers, satisfying shareholders, working collaboratively, developing talent and the numerous other demands placed on them.

One of the highest performing teams that I was fortunate to coach was Heathrow's Terminal Two (T2) Leadership Team. The team was accountable for the delivery of The Queen's Terminal, on time (4 June 2014) and on budget (£2.4bn). I had been coaching the team leader, Brian Woodhead, for a couple of years prior to him being offered the role and with a background in both the commercial and operational worlds he had a good perspective on what was required. He was very clear about his personal purpose which he articulated as, *"Being a maximizer."* Leading T2 certainly gave him the opportunity to maximize his potential!

For the first time in the history of Heathrow, Brian's boss assigned him a matrix team to deliver the terminal, which meant that the only way the team would succeed would be to work across the organization. The T2 leadership team consisted of 13 leaders with only two reporting directly to Brian, with the rest having a dotted line into him. Some members of the team had been peers to Brian and, being quite a hierarchical organization at the time, this proved an immediate challenge.

When Brian took over people were already up against it with the looming deadline and pressures were running high. We discussed what could be the best approach to take and Brian decided to bring the team together for a workshop to start exploring why the team existed and to define its common purpose. You could cut the tension in the room with a knife when we kicked off. Some members clearly thought that it was a waste of time and an interruption to their busy schedule. I am very accustomed to a healthy scepticism and like to ensure that everyone has the opportunity to have a share of voice to create the right environment for co-creating ideas together.

People expected us to jump straight into action and focus on the long list of tasks the team had to deliver. However, Brian was clear that in the first instance the team needed to define its purpose, which would act as a unifying factor going forward. After an in-depth inquiry, exploring questions to draw out a purpose like, 'Why do we exist?' 'What is our real value?' 'What difference do we want to make?' 'What do we want to be known for?' the team came up with the following purpose: *"To inspire people to be the best they can be."* This was a purpose that unified everyone. It was simple and memorable. It went beyond the act of opening the terminal, which was a very tangible goal to achieve. It became the guiding light for the team which kept shining as they went on an extraordinary journey together.

On another occasion, I was asked to work with a senior executive team in the engineering sector who had done enough team building events to sink a battle ship! They were team weary and were reluctant to take another two days out of the office to navel gaze. I was very upfront with them at the outset and informed them that they were welcome to fire me at the end of the event if tangible value was not added. I have learned to stay very open minded during the creation of a purpose. The last thing any team needs is another corporate mantra that is meaningless and which simply creates more cynicism.

This particular executive team was a real mix. There were a couple of founding members from over 15 years ago, one of whom had left and come back. Some members were brand new to the company, and the leader had just transitioned into the role three months earlier. To kick-off the process I asked everyone to write down five words that they would like to associate with the team. I captured all the words on a flip chart and asked people to select their top three, down to their first preference. I used this as the basis for probing them to think about why they existed, what it meant to be a team and what they wanted to be remembered for. Through discussions and exploration, the team came up with a statement about creating a better future; however, one member pushed back on the idea of being overly future focused, which could take them away from the day-to-day. Eventually they landed on creating better outcomes, which went down well, but on further thought they realized that the primary reason for their existence was to work together. The purpose was clear: *"Creating better outcomes together."*

The team was proud of their work and there was a genuine buy-in to the purpose. They agreed to hold themselves accountable to it and use it as a filter for all decision making.

This proved extremely valuable going forward as they were constantly having to make trade-offs about resources, both financial and people, so focusing on creating better outcomes together became a good test.

A clear purpose unifies a team. It anchors them on what matters most when other pressures take over. It energizes and inspires a team to lift up, be constructive and remember their true value and why they exist in the first place.

CREATING BUSINESS DIFFERENTIATION

At the centre of a successful company lies
a powerful purpose

Great companies have great purposes. This is backed up by research which highlights the following reasons why leaders should create purpose-driven organizations:

1. **Attract and retain the best employees.** People are 1.4 times more engaged, 1.7 times more satisfied and 3 times more likely to stay when working for a company with a strong purpose (The Energy Project, *What is the Quality of Life at Work*, 2013).

2. **Build loyalty and trust with customers.** 89% of clients believe a purpose-driven company will deliver the highest quality products and services, 72% of global companies would recommend a company with a purpose and 84% of emerging market consumers make cause related purchases at least annually (Edelman, *The goodpurpose*® study, 2013).

3. **Increase returns for shareholders.** Purpose-led companies outperformed the S&P500 by 10 times between 1996 and 2011 (Raj Sisodia, *Firms of Endearment*, 2007). Meaningful brands connected to human well-being

outperformed the stock market by 120% in 2013 (Havas Media, *Meaningful Brands Index*, 2013).

4. **Create shared value – economic value and social value are not mutually exclusive.** Today's sophisticated business leader recognizes the concept of shared value. Companies can bring business and society back together by redefining their purpose to creating 'shared value'. This will help them to generate economic value in a way that also produces value for society by addressing its challenges. A shared value approach reconnects company success with social progress as noted in 'Creating Shared Value' by Michael Porter and Mark Kramer, *Harvard Business Review*, Jan/Feb 2011.

This is better demonstrated by looking at some of the world's most valuable brands (according to a study by Brand Finance published on 1 February 2017). This demonstrates how companies with a clearly defined purpose develop premium brand positions, attract the best talent and keep them motivated and outperform in their respective markets.

Google, at number 1, states its purpose as, *"To organize the world's information and make it universally accessible and useful."* With a monetary value of $109.5bn and over 3.5 billion searches per day, it is safe to say that Google is fulfilling its purpose.

Apple, at number 2, has gone with a practical purpose, *"Apple designs Macs, the best personal computers in the world, along with OS X, iLife, iWork and professional software. Apple leads the digital music revolution with its iPods and iTunes online store."* With a monetary value of $107.1bn and a customer following second to none, Apple lives its purpose.

Amazon, at number 3, has its success as the top internet retailing company in the world due, at least in part, to their unwavering commitment to their purpose and daily execution of it, *"To be the earth's most customer-centric company; to build a place where people can come to find and discover anything they might want to buy online."* Amazon's monetary value is $106.3bn as they continue to innovate at an accelerated rate.

It is essential for any company of any size to clearly define its reason for existence. Being clear on your own purpose, the purpose of your team and the purpose of your company are the starting points to lead with purpose.

CHAPTER 2

THE
DISCOVERY
OF
PURPOSE

DEFINING PERSONAL PURPOSE

Purpose creates possibility

What is a personal purpose? Is it a thing? A destination? An endgame? A journey? I was clueless. I didn't know what a purpose was, let alone my own purpose, but I was determined to find out. Back in my early 20s, having left the music world I was questioning my career direction, as well as trying to figure out the key criteria to make the big decisions about how I wanted to live my life. I embarked on a search for purpose that took me across the world, visiting ashrams in India, attending personal development courses in America and a lot in-between! It cost me a lot of money and confusion.

On one seminal moment I was in Lucknow, a large city in northern India and the capital of the state of Uttar Pradesh. I had been encouraged by some good friends in the UK to meet a teacher of self-inquiry known as Papaji. His morning class meant that I had to get up at 5am and make my way through the dusty streets to find his home. Along with a group of primarily Western people in search of purpose, I was filled with anticipation to see what I would learn. The teaching was predominantly done in a question and answer style. One question asked was about how to deal with a relationship dilemma. Papaji's response was to suggest that the person in distress should chase the individual down the street with a shoe! This did very little to satisfy my curiosity. From then on, the more I listened the more disillusioned I became. I looked around and wondered what I was doing. I made a quick exit, changed my flight and came back to London earlier than planned. Following my travels, numerous courses and books, I came to realize that in the final analysis there is no single definition of purpose, and it was up to me to define it for myself.

When I was asked by IHG® to deliver a leadership programme on purpose it forced me to define it clearly:

A personal purpose is an aspirational reason for being.
It inspires and guides your life.
It is a deep conviction about what is most important.
It shapes your mindset, behaviour and actions.
It has a timeless quality, which is beyond circumstance.
It provides the whole meaning and direction of your life.

In essence, your purpose is your big 'why', your ultimate raison d'être. Your reason for existence, innate to you and within your DNA.

There are a couple of other definitions which are powerful statements of purpose from two of the leading authors on the subject. Bill George is the former chairman and chief executive officer of Medtronic. As the senior fellow at Harvard Business School and author of *Discover Your True North*, George describes a personal purpose as:

"Knowing the 'True North' of your internal compass. Your True North represents who you are as a human being at your deepest level. It is your orienting point – your fixed point in a spinning world – that helps you stay on track."

Simon Sinek is the author of *Start with Why*, and his talk *How Great Leaders Inspire Action* is listed as the third most popular TED presentation of all time. His definition is: *"Your Why is the purpose, cause or belief that inspires you."*

Most people often confuse goals and achievements with purpose. However, your purpose is not a tangible thing, it is 'why' you do what you do. Growing up maybe you thought your purpose was to get good grades. Then maybe you thought your purpose was to get a boy or a girlfriend and look cool. Then maybe you thought your purpose was to climb the corporate ladder. Get married. Have children. Purchase a house, cars, holidays. It's all great stuff, but it's not your purpose. These are goals, i.e. 'what' you want to achieve.

Your purpose is not a value. A personal value is a deeply held belief in which you have an emotional investment and which influences your behaviour. Values tend to come from learned experiences. For example, a leader told me how at the age of eight they were walking home from school, found a pound coin on the pavement, went to their local shop and bought a bag of sweets. Upon arriving home, they were confronted by their mother who demanded to know where they got the sweets. When they explained about finding the pound, the mother walked them back to the shop, handed back the sweets, took the coin, marched them to the bank and handed it in. The child learned the values of honesty and integrity. Values shape 'how' you behave, but they are not your purpose.

The way I see it as shown in the following diagram is that your purpose is at the core of your existence. Wrapped around your purpose are your values, with your goals an extension of what you want. Your ability to join up your purpose (why), values (how) and goals (what) becomes like a golden thread running through every aspect of your work, life and relationships. It ensures that you are clear, on track and focused on what is most meaningful to you.

PURPOSE MODEL

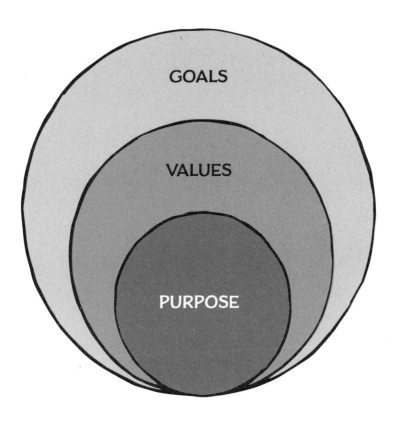

So, how do you know when you're on purpose? There are seven key principles that reveal if you're on purpose:

1. A purpose energizes.
2. A purpose strengthens resilience.
3. A purpose helps people be at their best.
4. A purpose enables creative flow.
5. A purpose ignites passion.
6. A purpose inspires.
7. A purpose connects authentically.

You certainly don't need to be in touch with all these characteristics on a consistent basis to be on purpose; however, paying attention to them will give you a good indication about whether you are on track or not.

DISCOVERING YOUR PURPOSE

Part of your life's journey is to discover your purpose.
Your life's joy is to live it.

I got a call from the Head of Talent of a major law firm. Jane knew me well and that I specialized in coaching leaders to discover their purpose. She said that one of her most talented lawyers was questioning his future and was looking for some support. Jane had asked if he would be willing to have a coaching session focused on his purpose. He had agreed and we set up a time to get together.

I met Stephen in central London and we found a quiet corner in a secluded hotel. He was extremely bright, quick thinking and personable. Stephen came straight to the point. He had been practising law his entire career, specializing in doing due diligence on major deals. But now, approaching his mid-forties, Stephen was reflecting on his future options. Should he stay in law, move into doing deals, enter the corporate world as General Counsel, take a risk and set up his own practice, or retrain in education and teach? I sensed quite a lot of confusion in Stephen and suggested exploring his purpose before looking at any external factors. I shared with him a definition of purpose and the steps he needed to take.

The starting point was to ask Stephen to think of the key activities in his life, and those which displayed him at his best.

When he was most fulfilled and why? When he was in flow and why? When he was experiencing 'peak' moments and why? Stephen sat back, sipped his coffee and reflected. He recounted the following memories:

- Growing up he loved playing sport. Any sport! The more the better. Soccer. Swimming. Tennis. Cycling. The vital question though was why? What was it about those activities that brought out the best in him? Stephen identified several themes – winning, competing, teamwork, having fun and testing his limits.

- Getting a 1st in his degree. Focusing on his academic achievement Stephen realized that this was to do with fulfilling his potential. He had applied himself wholeheartedly to his studies and, although he described himself as bright, it was the effort he put in that he felt most proud about.

- Pulling off his first deal. Stephen lit up when he described how he supported a big client in accomplishing a game-changing deal. As we explored this, Stephen recognized it was the element of helping others that had more significance than completing the transaction itself.

- Getting married. As Stephen discussed the memory of his wedding day, the stand out theme for him was connection and being surrounded by the people who meant the most to him in his life.

- Having children. A typical peak moment for many people, Stephen became visibly moved talking about the birth of his first daughter and, in particular, the courage of his wife who showed such remarkable determination during a difficult labour.

- Going on family holidays and camping. As he reminisced about trips he had taken with his family to the Dolomites and Pyrenees, he realized it was the sense of freedom and being inspired by nature that accompanied these experiences which meant so much to him.

We then summarized the main themes emerging from his key experiences in order to explore any linkages or patterns they had in common. Stephen highlighted the following ten themes:

1. Winning;
2. Teamwork;
3. Freedom;
4. Beauty;
5. Learning;
6. Application;
7. Helping others;
8. Connection;
9. Courage;
10. Fun.

I asked him to group them under some broader headings, which he identified as:

1. Relationship – connection, helping others and teamwork;
2. Achievement – winning, application, learning and courage;
3. Creativity – freedom, beauty and fun.

Stephen then explored which out of these three categories meant the most to him. He said relationship. We continued the exploration with the following inquiry:

Ben: What is it about relationship that is so meaningful to you?

Stephen: Making a difference in people's lives. I derive great satisfaction from working in teams and helping others achieve their goals.

Ben: If you are making a difference in people's lives, and helping them achieve their goals, then what?

Stephen: I am adding value.

Ben: What value do you want to add?

Stephen: To help people achieve their potential and be the best they can be.

Ben: Why?

Stephen: Because then I feel that I have stretched myself in helping others and learned more about myself.

Ben: What do you really want to learn about yourself?

Stephen: The truth about myself. Who I am really. What I am capable of. What is the best version of me.

Ben: If you knew the truth about yourself then what?

Stephen: I would be fulfilled!

Ben: Would it be true to say that your purpose has to do with knowing yourself and being the best version of you?

Stephen: Yes, however I feel more strongly about being the best I can be, than knowing myself.

Ben: OK, what if your purpose is to be the best you can be?

Stephen: That resonates. If I was being the best I can be, then I would fulfil my potential. I would stretch myself. I would be energized. I would be resilient. I could apply it to being a father, husband, son, lawyer, partner ... in fact any activity.

Through this shared dialogue, together we identified some important indicators that revealed Stephen was in the right place, and in line with his purpose. He found that it was:

- Consistent – he could apply his purpose to all areas of his work, life and relationships.

- Energizing – he was fuelled by the idea of it and it ignited passion.

- Fulfilling – he knew that by being on purpose he would thrive.

- Significant – he recognized that his purpose linked him to what was most valuable.

There is no one set formula for landing on your purpose. I tell my clients it took me 20 years, so to discover it in two hours makes me realize I'm a slow learner! However, if someone is ready, open minded and prepared to be challenged, then it is possible to dig deep and get to the heart of the matter.

I asked Stephen what would happen if he applied his purpose to his current career dilemma. We started by exploring what it would look like if Stephen was following his purpose and being the best he could be in law. He said it would mean the following:

- Doing big deals;
- Playing a leadership role;
- Making a strategic contribution to the firm;
- Exercising great judgment;
- Developing others;
- Supporting his family.

I challenged him to consider what it would be like if becoming more purpose-led was the next step for his career. What would happen if he was truly being the best he could be every day at the firm? Stretching himself to be the best leader? The best strategic thinker? The best at developing others? The best at supporting his family?

Stephen stood up at the close of our two hours and thanked me profusely for helping him take a very different view about his purpose and situation. He was committed to continuing the process and we agreed that he would let me know about his next steps. From a personal perspective, it was hugely gratifying to observe Stephen move from confusion to clarity within a short amount of time on something as significant as purpose and to understand the impact that it would have on his future career.

IDENTIFYING YOUR PURPOSE

Know your purpose, know yourself

Identifying your purpose is one of the most important acts you can take in life. It never ceases to amaze me how many accomplished people have yet to define the very essence of who they are. However, the gift of knowing your purpose lies in your hands. By committing to a journey of revisiting peak experiences, i.e. when you have been at your best, most fulfilled, in flow, inspired and connected, it will show you the way to purpose.

The specific steps to take in identifying your purpose are as follows:

1. Record the peak moments from your life so far, i.e. times when you have been at your best, most fulfilled, in flow.

2. Reflect upon what was happening, what activities you were doing that made the event a highlight, e.g. travel, sports, work, creativity, charitable, relational.

3. Identify the key themes linked with your peak moments, e.g. freedom, learning, giving, innovating, achieving.

4. Group the themes into broader categories, e.g. making a difference, helping people, making change happen.

5. Identify a category that stands out.

6. Ask a trusted partner to help you explore your stand out theme in more depth using questions such as:
   a. What does your theme mean to you and why?
   b. If you were to achieve your theme then what?
   c. What would be the ultimate end point of your theme?
   d. What difference would it make to you if you were to realize your theme?

7. Ask your trusted confidant to playback to you what they have heard and summarize a potential purpose by saying, 'Would it be true if …?'

8. Clarify an initial purpose statement in a way that is meaningful to you.

My recommendation is to set aside at least an hour of uninterrupted time and use the table opposite to record your answers:

PURPOSE FRAMEWORK

PEAK MOMENTS	You at your best, most fulfilled, in flow, inspired and connected with what is most meaningful to you
ACTIVITY	Activities you were doing that made an event a peak experience
THEMES	Key theme that you associated with a peak experience
CATEGORIES	Themes grouped into broader areas
STAND OUT	What has the biggest pull for you
PURPOSE	Initial purpose statement

As you explore your purpose, you need to be aware, and ensure you are not being vague in your thoughts. For instance:

- With statements like, 'To make a difference', 'To add value', 'To leave a legacy', you need to ask yourself, 'What difference do you want to make?' 'What value do you want to add?' 'What legacy do you want to leave?' You need to keep probing and go deeper than the initial motivation expressed.

- Make a distinction between a 'means' and an 'end-state'. If you say that your purpose is to 'make others' lives better', think about what it would mean if you were to do this. Is it the act of making others' lives better that brings you genuine fulfilment or, for instance, the possibilities that emerge from making others' lives better? Which of these is the ultimate end-game and therefore has a greater impact?

- Keep it simple. Sometimes the most powerful purposes are the simplest ones. There is no such thing as a right purpose. There is your purpose, which you must resonate with.

- Don't be surprised if your purpose feels selfish. Innate within every purpose are the seeds to help others. For example, if your purpose is to be happy, studies from social science show that happy people are selfless and have more to give. Unhappy people are more selfish and have less to give.

- You have one core purpose which translates into every role and all aspects of your life. You purpose is consistent for your family and work. However, the way it manifests itself will be different subject to the situation.

Example of purpose statements:

> *"Live in a way that respects and enhances*
> *the freedom of others."*
> Nelson Mandela

> *"Make a dent in the universe."*
> Steve Jobs

> *"Live your best life."*
> Oprah Winfrey

> *"Unlock the gifts of every person around the world."*
> Mark Zuckerberg

Purpose statements from some of the leaders I have worked with include:

> *Be a creator of opportunity*
> *Make big things happen*
> *Achieve the unimaginable*
> *Help others succeed and fulfil their dreams*
> *Be significant*
> *Be the best I can be*
> *Art of the possible*
> *Be love*
> *Be happy*

The main ingredient to defining your purpose is to be willing. Keep an open mind. Don't rush. Your purpose is precious. Give yourself the gift of time and space to clarify the essence of you.

LIVING YOUR
VALUES

Values show what you believe

It's important to have awareness about the difference between your values and purpose. Often, I find people are clear about their values but make a mistake by trying to put them together to form their purpose. A personal value is a deeply held belief which shapes your behaviour. Values are derived from the major turning points, events and experiences that have shaped your life, since it is these that form your deepest learnings and conclusions.

There are a range of values, which become intensely personal to us. These are shown in the diagram opposite:

VALUES FRAMEWORK

Relationship values
· Trust
· Respect
· Diversity
· Inclusion
· Teamwork
· Collaboration
· Compassion

Integrity values
· Doing the right thing
· Openness & honesty
· Fairness
· Safety
· Work ethic
· Responsibility
· Discipline

Success values
· Aim high
· Achievement
· Performance
· Results
· Delivery
· Recognition
· Power

Happiness values
· Love
· Freedom
· Fulfilment
· Fun
· Humour
· Joy
· Creativity

In order to define your values, you first need to uncover the major events from your life, identify the impact of each event, highlight the key learning and clarify the value shaped. Often, when people define their values they'll find that although they know what these are, they are not clear about the influencing factors that have shaped them.

As an example, four key events from my life and relevant impact, lessons learned and my core values are illustrated in the table below:

Event	Aged eight, my family uprooted from a beautiful home in Leeds, Yorkshire to head down South to Surrey, where my father took up the headship of the Yehudi Menuhin School. I had loved living in Leeds, as not only did I support Leeds United, but as a family we enjoyed uninterrupted time playing in the garden, or walking in the Yorkshire moors. When my parents took over the boarding school, our family was disrupted. I distinctly remember lying in bed at night, waiting for my parents to come and say goodnight, but, by the time they had done the rounds with 45 other children, I was asleep.
Impact	Sense of loss as a result of my parents reduced ability to give attention
Learning	Children need parents' active love and attention to enjoy healthy development
Value	Love

Event	Aged 16, I suffered a major shock. I had attended an Outward-Bound course in the English Lake District, a beautiful part of the world. I arrived back home in peak fitness, following several weeks of mountain and rock climbing, canoeing and other outdoor activities. Upon walking in the door, I was greeted by my mother who was extremely upset. Through her tears, she informed me that the marriage had broken down. It was a difficult time as we had to return to the school and keep up appearances until my parents worked through their separation, which took several months.
Impact	The bewilderment of everything I had taken for granted being turned upside down
Learning	Expect the unexpected
Value	Honesty

Event	I continued with my violin studies and, upon leaving school, secured my place at the Guildhall School of Music and Drama. However, before starting college I took a gap year. This was pretty much unheard of in the music world, where the norm was to keep practising in the fear that you might lose your finesse. One of the adventures I took was to join a kibbutz in Israel. At the age of 18, I distinctly remember leaving the cold and wet of England in early January and arriving in sunny Tel Aviv. I had a few hours before my flight so headed down to the beach with my backpack and violin. I will never forget sitting down on the sand, looking over at the Mediterranean Sea and having an overwhelming sense of freedom.
Impact	Recognition that there was more to life than playing the violin!
Learning	The need to broaden my horizons and take some risks
Value	Freedom

Event	By my mid-twenties, I had reached a point where I was happily single. Following several heartbreaks, I decided to enjoy my independence and not consider marriage until later in life. The universe had other plans for me. I met Veronica briefly in London through mutual friends who invited her to one of my public courses. She was from New Zealand and living in Tokyo at the time. It was a fleeting connection, which was followed up a year later by some mutual friends who came back from Tokyo and mentioned her to me. I called her up and she vaguely remembered who I was. After a few months of an evolving, expensive long-distance friendship, I asked her if she wanted to join me and some friends on a trip to India for the summer. Veronica came over with her best girlfriend. We met outside the Bahá'í Temple in New Delhi, which is a stunning building in the shape of a lotus leaf. We then took off for a road trip in Rajasthan and, within three days of being together, all I could think of was marriage and babies! It completely freaked me out. However, after another three weeks travelling, I knew that our future would be together.
Impact	Falling in love when I least expected it
Learning	The universe works in mysterious ways
Value	Connection

By working through the following exercise, you can clarify your values and understand their origins. Through completing this process, you will understand the difference between your personal purpose and values.

Find a quiet spot and set aside approximately one hour. As you do the exercise you will probably find that most of the major turning points from your life have to do with adversity, so it's best to do this when you won't be interrupted:

1. Draw a horizontal line across a page. This represents the duration of your life to date.

2. Below the line, chronologically mark the key experiences and turning points that have shaped your life so far, e.g. birth of a sibling, school, relationships, higher education, location changes, job changes, relationships with line managers, work failings, financial issues, redundancy, family matters, deaths.

3. Against each event note the impact that it had on you, e.g. sense of loss, betrayal, injustice, failure, incompetence, frustration, anger, fear, sadness.

4. Reflect upon the learning you gained, or conclusion made from the impact, e.g. honesty is the best policy, moving homes makes you resilient, failing at school can be a motivating factor, poor line management drives you to be a great leader, redundancy can liberate you, death makes you appreciate life.

5. Identify the specific value linked to the experience, e.g. honesty, optimism, respect, fairness, learning.

LIFELINE EXERCISE

EVENT	EVENT	EVENT	EVENT
IMPACT	IMPACT	IMPACT	IMPACT
LEARNING	LEARNING	LEARNING	LEARNING
VALUE	VALUE	VALUE	VALUE

It is essential to be clear about your values and where they came from so that you can stay true to what is most important for you. From a leadership perspective being clear about your values breeds trust and putting your values alongside your purpose inspires belief.

IDENTIFYING
TEAM PURPOSE

A shared purpose sits at the heart of a great team

As leader of a team, or as a team member, you need to be able to answer the following critical questions:

- Why does your team exist?
- What is the big why of your team?
- What is the unifying North Star of your team?
- What is the real value of your team?
- What difference do you want to make as a team?

I believe that it is important for a team to discover its core purpose, to provide vital clarity about why a team exists and to foster a sense of identity as a unifying factor. However, this has to be an authentic process and I make no assumptions that either a team will want to create a purpose, or follow it. There is nothing worse than a team going through the motions of generating a purpose to please the leader when there is no genuine buy-in or commitment.

I had been asked to facilitate a brand and marketing team offsite. The team consisted of extremely capable and experienced professionals and my pre-meeting conversations with each team member alerted me to the fact that they were busy and not overly keen about having to take two days out of the office. I was familiar with the scenario and warned the leader that the stakes were high, therefore we needed to ensure it was a game-changing event. Fiona, the team leader, reminded me that although each team member performed highly in their own area, the only way that they could deliver the entirety of the commercial plan was by leveraging the power of the collective and working together as a team. This would enable them to progress a series of initiatives including reducing cost, sharing talent, creating a better working environment and providing consistent leadership.

Fiona opened the event with clear a message for the team about the importance of the two-days. However, she was quick to point out that the only way it would work was if everyone was open and honest in their communication. Fiona highlighted the fact that she was under no illusion about the nature of the conversations we were about to embark upon, as well as agreeing that nothing would be taken forward unless the team believed in the value of it. The last thing this team needed was another to-do list!

What quickly emerged in our first conversation about the current team's effectiveness was an issue about the team's engagement in a similar offsite a couple of years previously. Although a lot of energy had been generated at the time, there had been no follow through on the commitments made, and the purpose statement they had created was now meaningless. I requested that before continuing with our agenda, we needed to address the 'elephant in the room' – if the team believed that they should either operate as a collective, or stay in their existing silos.

I asked everyone to write down their top pros and cons of being in a team, and collected the following insights:

Pros for being a team
- Boosting resilience for overcoming challenges;
- Developing talent;
- Improving ability to deliver;
- Sharing best practice;
- Providing mutual support;
- Demonstrating cooperation vs. competition;
- Unleashing energy, enthusiasm and fun.

Cons for being a team
- Losing individual team identities;
- Deprioritizing individual team priorities;
- Spending time on team culture;
- Taking away time for work;
- Setting ourselves up to fail as a result of not following through;
- Achieving outcomes which might go against personal choice.

As a result of this conversation the team recognized the power of being in a team and agreed to validate it over the following two days. This was an important outcome which meant that we now had a real opportunity to define an authentic purpose. To do this, I asked each team member to write down five words that they associated with the team. Sometimes these words need to be aspirational if the team is not in a healthy place. Alternatively, it may be a case of drawing out the best of the team in a clearly articulated way.

On this occasion, the words people shared included:

Success. Performance. Inspire. Leadership. Talent. Growth. Effectiveness. Engagement. Delivery. Commitment. Cohesion. Trust. Accountability. Honesty. Love. Fun. Results.

I wrote the list of words on a white board and then gave everyone three votes to allocate to their preferred words. The outcome was:

1. Inspire;
2. Love;
3. Growth.

I then conducted an inquiry to help the team define their end state – why did they exist? They landed on the purpose: *"To inspire love."* From an internal perspective, they agreed that as a leadership team their ultimate value was to inspire their people to perform and that love expressed their desire to create a great place to work, where people could do what they love in a way they loved doing it. From an external perspective, to inspire love meant connecting with customers in a meaningful way that built connections and ensured the brand added real value in their lives. The purpose was simple, clear and memorable which meant that it had a chance to stick.

On another occasion, I worked with a commercial leadership team. The team had endured a fractured past with intense rivalry, back biting and fighting for resources which had soured the department over several years. The leader was new to the team, and wanted to give some members of the team a chance to change before making decisions about their future roles. This team were even more cynical about aligning on a purpose than the previous one I mentioned, however, we went through a similar exercise and they discovered *"Grow revenue to grow the company"* as their purpose.

In situations like this, when a purpose is identified, my advice is to live with it for at least 90-days before making any formal communication to others. It is all too common for teams to come back enthused from an offsite, making grand statements about all the changes they are going to instigate for the better, only for a week later everything going back to the status quo under the pressure of day-to-day delivery.

The commercial team agreed to live with the purpose for three months to see if it had currency, and if it would provide a true North Star. After the 90 days we got back together to test its value. People shared stories about how the purpose had caught their attention and that it had definitely enabled them to think more broadly, as well as energized them to drive revenue. They decided that the purpose could provide a valuable sense of identity for the department and agreed to launch it at their next department quarterly review meeting. Bringing the entire function together was a risk because there were still many unspokens between different pockets in the department. However, the leader was bold and realized that unless the leadership team started to shift the collective mindset they could go backwards. The team designed an engaging meeting that would provide an opportunity for everyone to share a point of view about why they existed as a commercial function. Both revenue and growth surfaced as key touchpoints, which meant that the leadership team were then in a position to reveal their draft purpose: *"Grow revenue to grow the company."* They were pleasantly surprised by the wider team welcoming it with open arms. It showed that they were yearning for a deeper meaning about why they did what they did, as well as providing a clear unified direction.

Purpose statements from some other teams that I have coached include:

Lead the business
– Executive Committee

Kick Ass Technology Team (KATT)
– Technology Leadership Team

To create better outcomes together
– Operational Leadership Team

Better journeys for a better company
– Customer Services Leadership Team

Communicate love
– Communications Leadership Team

Inspire people to be the best they can be
– HR Leadership Team

I believe that every team has a core purpose and it is the responsibility of a team leader to at least give their team an opportunity to explore what it is. If done well, a shared purpose will inspire a team to go in the same direction; it will engage hearts and minds and it will give a deeper sense of meaning about why the team exists beyond delivering a set of objectives.

CLARIFYING ORGANIZATIONAL PURPOSE

*Great companies know why they exist
beyond shareholder return*

At its best, an organizational purpose provides the necessary focus and direction for people to follow. It is the True North for a company which enables clear decision making to take place. It gives a sense of meaning that people can get behind and identify with. It is the reason why a company exists and is an aspirational call to arms.

At its worst, an organizational purpose is simply a corporate slogan which has no emotional connection for people and is therefore given lip service. Even more damaging is when companies have done the exact opposite of what they proclaim through deadly actions. For example, Enron's purpose statement was, *"Respect, Integrity, Communication and Excellence."* But in October 2001, Enron collapsed. At the time this was the biggest corporate bankruptcy to ever hit the financial world due to accounting and corporate fraud.

Lehman Brothers purpose statement was, *"To build unrivalled partnerships with and value for our clients, through the knowledge, creativity and dedication of our people, leading to superior returns to our shareholders."* On 15 September 2008, Lehman Brothers filed for bankruptcy, which became the largest in history.

It is no surprise when I ask people about their company purpose statement that I often encounter rolling eyes. It's a breeding ground for sceptics. However, the absence of an authentic purpose gives rise to a lack of unity about why a company exists, which can cause confusion and disengagement.

When done well, the opportunity to clarify an organizational purpose is a big engagement exercise, allowing the majority of people a chance to contribute to defining the company's DNA.

I was working with the executive committee of a leading retailer in technology. The company was experiencing a turbulent time as it was being hit by the might of Amazon and the need for digital transformation. The executives were keen to get back to their roots and redefine why the company started in the first place. They had a large offsite scheduled with their top 100 colleagues and wanted to form a point of view about their organizational purpose. We scheduled a day in a relaxed environment to ensure they were in the right frame of mind for this event. We started with a discussion about purpose to ensure they were aligned on the need to invest in creating a refreshed purpose. Their previous one read, *"To make sure we put the customer first, always."* This had been somewhat successful in engaging colleagues, however, it was perceived as out of date and did not have currency in the business.

I shared with them some purpose statements from other organizations to stimulate thinking:

To refresh the world in mind, body and spirit. Coca-Cola

We create happiness by providing the best in entertainment for people of all ages everywhere. Walt Disney

Bring the world closer together. Facebook

To create a better everyday life for the many people. IKEA

Believe in better. Sky

I asked the executives to individually write down statements that demonstrated why the company existed, what made it special, what made it unique and what made it different. Key themes that came out of this process included:

- Providing solutions for customers;
- Giving advice to improve customer lives;
- Connecting customers with what they want;
- Making products and services accessible;
- Ensuring customers have a memorable experience.

As we explored these themes in more depth I asked them to dig deeper asking: Why provide solutions for customers? Why give advice and connect customers with what they want? Why ensure customers have a memorable experience? Although they might seem obvious answers, it's critical to have the conversation to ensure everyone is on the same page. Eventually an idea emerged that seemed to really capture attention: *"To make lives easier."*

With this in mind we did a similar exercise at the top 100 event. I had each executive facilitate a table of ten colleagues. They were under strict instructions to not plant their ideas and to allow the core truth about the company to emerge. Remarkably, the idea about making lives easier surfaced again. People loved the idea that the reason for the company's existence was to make colleagues', customers' and shareholders' lives easier. This made a lot of sense as a provider of technology because they could clearly see how their efforts could make a tangible difference.

We validated the purpose against the seven key principles required to make a purpose successful:

1. **A purpose energizes.** Making lives easier definitely energized people to go the extra mile in a complex world.

2. **A purpose strengthens resilience.** Everyone agreed that in the case of setbacks, making lives easier would help them to bounce back quickly.

3. **A purpose helps people be at their best.** People could see the linkage between how being at their best would enable making lives easier.

4. **A purpose enables creative flow.** The commitment to making lives easier encouraged people to think differently and come up with innovative solutions.

5. **A purpose ignites passion.** Everyone got fired up by the idea of making lives easier.

6. **A purpose inspires.** In very competitive trading conditions the focus of making lives easier lifted people's spirits.

7. **A purpose connects in an authentic way.** Given the fact that the company was in existence to make lives easier, this was a natural focus to follow.

The purpose ticked all the required boxes and, as a result, the executive committee agreed to embed it in their company culture.

Whatever the stage of organizational development, it is valuable to either redefine the purpose to ensure it is current and meaningful; refresh the purpose if it needs new energy and visibility; or, if you are in the early days of forming a company, then it is the perfect time to start with purpose.

CHAPTER 3

A
PURPOSE
MINDSET

A MINDSET
SHIFT

Your life is an outcome of your mindset

Now that you have greater clarity about why purpose matters and what it is, and you have started to identify your own personal purpose, it is critical to draw your attention to the importance of your mindset and the impact it has on leading with purpose.

Our mindset is an established set of attitudes we hold. Through the study of neuroscience, using magnetic resonance imaging (MRI) and other imaging techniques, we can now study the structures and functions of the brain in real time. Recent advances have shown that the brain is far more malleable than we ever knew. These new understandings give us deeper insights into how we develop our mindset, what obstacles prevent us from having the type of attitudes we would like and that with practice, neural networks grow new connections leading to new mindsets.

In this chapter, we will explore some profound mindset shifts required for you to be able to translate your purpose into a day-to-day experience. The following are important distinctions that we will explore:

- **Doing**: A mindset which has become conditioned to focus on transaction and task.

- **Having**: A mindset fixed on the accumulation and consumption of possessions.

- **Being**: A mindset based on your essential nature that connects you with your authentic self.

- **Choice**: Our ability to choose our mindset in any given situation, which determines how we respond to events.

- **Intention**: The opportunity to deliberately develop our mindset in conscious ways. At the core of a purpose mindset is the intention to be purpose-led.

DOING
TO BEING

We are called human beings,
not human doings for a reason

When you wake up in the morning what is on your mind? Typical responses include:

- The kids;
- Tea or coffee?
- The traffic;
- The weather;
- The inbox;
- Meetings;
- What am I going to wear?
- Where do I need to be?
- What crises happened overnight?

You've got to admit, it's an inspiring list! There is one thing these thoughts have in common ... tasks. Even morning thoughts about the kids tend to be associated with getting them up, school and unfinished homework. More specifically it is a 'to-do' list.

Having asked thousands of leaders around the world what is on their mind in the morning, I can categorically say that the majority of people operate on 'autopilot'. The good news is that there are multiple benefits of habituated responses.

Brain researchers estimate that the human mind takes in 11 million pieces of information per second through our senses. Our brain is consciously aware of only approximately 40 of them. The unconscious mind, which operates on autopilot, manages the rest. The brain creates 'mental shortcuts' to help us interpret information faster and save energy in making decisions. Therefore, upon awakening we can whip through the non-essentials without having to drain energy. However, the outcome will be repetitive and the risk is that we lean towards becoming 'human doings', rather than 'human beings'.

As an alternative to a 'doing mindset', there is a different mindset – a 'being mindset', orchestrated by the question, 'How do you want to be?'

In order to make the shift from doing to being the challenge we have to overcome is based on the following approach:

MINDSET SHIFT

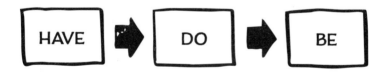

We tell ourselves that when we 'have' what we think we want, we will 'do' what we think we want and then 'be' the kind of person we want. This is a big mistake and backward thinking.

I was coaching a chief financial officer (CFO) of a public company. Just about to turn 50, David's grandfather had been a coal miner and his father a professional footballer. Unfortunately, his father had broken his back in a motorbike accident and, as a consequence, had to re-educate himself to get back on a career track. David had learned a work ethic which drove him. Aware of the sacrifices his ancestors had made, David had a mindset based on the following: *"If I do enough work, I can have financial security and be happy when I retire."* I challenged David on this unconsciously crafted mindset. Was this really the best logic to drive his future? Particularly as his father had died within 18 months of retiring; not an uncommon occurrence.

In our work David had arrived at his purpose, *"To be the best I can be."* This really inspired him and he could see how he could apply it as a husband, father, CFO, leader and team player. In light of this, was waiting until retirement to be happy really the best strategy? He agreed it wasn't; however, he was perplexed about how to make a shift.

I encouraged him to consider an alternative approach:

MINDSET SHIFT

BE → DO → HAVE

Be the person you want to be and let it shape and influence what you do and have.

As the milestone of turning 50 loomed I challenged David to consider what his life would look like if he was being purpose-led, in other words being the best he could be? He could immediately see that postponing happiness for another 10 years was not on the cards. He asked himself, *"What if I committed to being the best I can be every day?"* His responses included:

- I would be there for my teenage children who are struggling with their exams, rather than waiting until it's too late and they've left home.

- I would re-engage with my wife and focus on rebuilding our life together, rather than waiting until the kids have left and then trying to fill the void.

- I would be more challenging at Exec meetings, rather than sitting back and letting others dominate the debate.

- I would step up as a team leader and inspire my team to provide better financial guidance to the business, rather than accepting average performance.

- I would actively network and accept invitations to connect with other professionals, rather than always telling myself I'm too busy.

- I would get back on my bike and complete L'Étape du Tour, which lets thousands of amateur cyclists race over the same route as a Tour de France, rather than wait until it's too late.

David went off to put his new mindset into action. I met with him shortly after he had completed L'Étape du Tour. David described how upon climbing the highest peak of the ride, and being slightly ahead of his teammates, he stopped to take in the view. He was overcome with emotion. Surveying the natural beauty, David had a deep realization that he did not need to wait 10 years to be the person he really wanted to be. It was a choice that lay in his hands today. By shifting his mindset, he could be purpose-led and stop putting his 'to-do' list at the top of his priorities.

This is a vital point I make to leaders. You will always have a 'to-do' list. Even when you die there will be a list. But the big question is, how do you want 'to be'? The invitation is to put your 'to be' at the top of your 'to do'.

THE AWARENESS
OF CHOICE

Life happens, but you choose how you respond

Probably the biggest breakthrough in psychology in the last century was the recognition that in-between a stimulus and a response there is a choice. This insight was brought home to me most acutely through the extraordinary work of Victor Frankl. In his momentous book, *Man's Search for Meaning*, Frankl made the profound statement, *"Everything can be taken from a man but one thing: the last of the human freedoms – to choose one's attitude in any given set of circumstances, to choose one's own way."*

Life happens; however, we choose our response to life happening, the outcome of our choices will determine how life impacts us. For instance, consciously choosing how we want to be will have a major influence on how we show up and what we do.

The president of Americas for a global company, Hugh was a big advocate of the power of choice and encouraged his team and employees to embrace it wholeheartedly. For instance, on a Monday morning when many people were getting up to speed after the weekend, Hugh would deliberately thank people for choosing to come to work. This would leave many perplexed as they hadn't been thanked for simply showing up, but Hugh would go on to explain that he recognized they had choices. They were choosing to serve this particular organization vs. the competitors. They were choosing to give of their time vs. being with their families. He would thank his team for attending his meetings and recognize their commitment to working together vs. operating in silos. This approach had a massive impact on engagement and reflected in the overall company employee engagement scores, plus the loyalty people showed to Hugh through his followership was legendary.

Do the choices you make move you in the direction you want to go? Psychologists estimate that we think about 70,000 thoughts a day. That's a lot of thoughts. It works out at about 3,000 thoughts per hour, or 50 per minute. Each thought has the potential to turn into a choice. We either have the option to make conscious choices or not. What I've noticed in my work is that if we're not making smart choices it's because there are blocks getting in the way.

On one of my senior leadership development programmes about diversity and inclusion, we focus on helping people learn how to appreciate difference. In the session, we explore the notion of bias, both conscious and unconscious. On one occasion a delegate spoke up about a conscious bias she had of 'lazy people'. There was a majority of nodding heads in the group as people agreed with the dislike of others not putting in effort. My bias was to agree, but I checked myself and challenged the leader to consider the idea that it is rare for people to arrive at work deliberately choosing to be lazy and underperform. My experience is that if someone is failing to deliver, there is a reason, and before making any assumptions it's critical to learn what is stopping someone from fulfilling their potential. I challenged the group to consider what could be going on that would result in evidence of laziness. They came up with examples including:

- Personal challenges at home;
- Lack of competence and skill to perform a task;
- Lack of motivation and desire due to an issue with a line manager or colleague;
- Disagreeing with the strategic or cultural direction of an organization.

I pointed out that we need to become highly conscious about the thoughts we entertain since these lead to the choices we make. Thinking someone is lazy causes us to choose to ignore, avoid or tolerate the individual, rather than seeking to understand what is going on. How do you feel and respond if someone is ignoring, avoiding or tolerating you? You wouldn't be at your best and as a leader it certainly won't help you enable someone to identify and overcome whatever blocks are in their way to lift their performance.

Becoming conscious of the choices you make is an important skill to develop given the impact of them. It stops you from reacting to life as a passenger, and puts you firmly in the driving seat. When you embrace the idea that everything is a choice it brings freedom. Rather than rallying against events happening, you learn to choose your response in considered ways. In a world of such massive unpredictability and uncertainty your ability to choose your own way becomes an essential imperative to rise to challenges and thrive. It enables you to be proactive in situations and is an imperative for choosing to lead with purpose.

THE POWER
OF INTENTION

Intention inspires outcome

Alongside choice, there is one further consideration which is instrumental in shaping mindset – intention. Every action, thought and feeling we have is motivated by an intention, and that intention is a cause which creates an effect. As a consequence, every intention we set, either consciously or unconsciously, has an outcome. In this most profound way we are held responsible for our every action, thought and feeling, which is to say, for our every intention. We intend something to be and within intention lies the seeds of creation.

For instance, we can intend to grow through life, or go through life. We can intend to inspire others, or endure others. We can intend to create new possibilities, or copy others. We can intend to lead with purpose, or let ourselves be led. Our intention will make it so.

The first book I wrote was called *Successful But Something Missing*. The book was based on my life and career up until that point which consisted primarily of pursuing goals, but experiencing a void. I could tell you what I thought success would look like once I had ticked off everything on my list but, in the meantime, I struggled with defining success on a daily basis. It was time to take my own medicine so I set a conscious intention to be successful every day. This was such a foreign concept to me I had to take a series of practical steps to make it possible.

The first action I took was to write every morning in my personal journal the intention to be successful today. Not tomorrow, not when I had achieved my goals, but today. I then asked myself, *"How would I know at the end of the day if I had been successful or not?"* I wrote down three key success measures that would enable me to define success for the day, for example:

1. To inspire delegates attending my leadership programmes;
2. To help leaders discover their core purpose;
3. To be present with my children once I got home.

With this intention set in motion I would then discipline myself during the day to make deliberate choices to support my intention. I would choose to exercise daily as I knew this would energize me and ensure I was in a more inspired state when delivering my programmes. I would choose to listen with deep compassion to clients so that they felt understood. I would choose to play with my kids once getting home, rather than to collapse on the sofa!

The outcome was that my relationship with success shifted. I embraced it every day, rather than simply believing that it was an outcome of task. Success became a mindset based on a deliberate intention to be successful.

Rob was a formidable salesman. As Director of Sales & Acquisition for a major media company he operated in probably the most aggressive company culture I have witnessed. When we kicked-off our coaching programme Rob was obsessed by a number that he was targeted to deliver. The company reputation with investors and analysts rested on him hitting this target. For Rob, the stakes were high both at work and home. Married with two young children, Rob was rarely home. When he did make it back, he was so shattered that Rob could barely keep awake and if he did get home he was in a foul mood. The ultimatum came from his wife. Change or the marriage was over. Rob was a chain smoker. He believed it kept him sane. Then the ultimatum came from the company doctor. Quit, or risk serious health consequences. The triple whammy came when I conducted a feedback exercise with his colleagues and the message came back loud and clear. Stop being a corporate bully, or his colleagues would stop collaborating with him and his number was doomed.

Where to start? Intention. Rob agreed to engage in a coaching exercise that required him to fast forward to the end of his life and look back. What did he want to see, feel and hear at his own funeral? I asked Rob to write the eulogy that he would like to be shared about the difference he had made in life, work, family and society. It was a breakthrough moment. Nowhere in his reflections were comments about smashing targets at any cost, breaking up his family and accelerating his own death due to poor health habits. What did emerge was his intention to be a great leader respected for his ability to develop others, inspire performance and work in a highly collaborative way. As a father, Rob recognized that his true intent was to be a loving, supportive and fun parent who played an active role in bringing up his children. As a husband, Rob confessed that his intention was to honour his marriage and do whatever was necessary to nurture the light in his partnership, no matter how dark the flame had gone. Rob went further and wrote that ultimately his intention was to be inspired by a purpose which he described as, *"Making the world a better place."*

Having considered the end, we came back to the here and now and conducted another exercise to map out the next three years of intention. I asked Rob to focus on the next 12 months. What intention did he want to have? *"To be present."* In two years what would his intention be? *"To be inspired."* In three years how would he describe his intent? *"To be free."* We then broke each intention into a set of clear success measures evidencing how he would know it would be true. This became his road map to guide his choices going forward.

Rob surprised himself with the outcomes. He gave up smoking virtually overnight. When I asked what made the difference, after numerous attempts to stop over the years, he said that the intention to be present was the wake-up call. He could not be present if he smoked. It gave him the fortitude to resist the urge to smoke, go through withdrawal and quit. He worked with his PA to reschedule his calendar ensuring he got home on time twice a week to read his kids precious bedtime stories. He enlisted the support of his parents one Sunday a month to look after the children so that he could invest in rebuilding his marriage. He surprised his team and peers by reaching out for help, asking for guidance about his plans to hit the numbers and showing willingness to evolve his plans in real time, thereby making the necessary changes to go on and outperform.

Intention is a leadership muscle that you need to exercise daily. I recommend you ask yourself the following types of questions to keep you on track:

- What is your intention today?
- What is your intention for the meeting you are about to run or participate in?

- What is your intention for the conversation you are about to have?
- What is your intention for the presentation you are about to give?
- What is your intention as a friend?
- What is your intention as a parent?
- What is your intention as a partner?
- What is your intention as a community member?
- What is your intention as a leader?
- What is your intention for running a business?
- What is your intention as a human being?

An example of how to use such answers is found through how Oprah Winfrey's television show changed and developed. As she says, *"The number one principle that rules my life is intention."* Her bottom-line intention, she reveals, is to be a force for good in the world. Following an episode that went awry after inviting members of the Kl Klux Klan on to the show to discover the roots of their hatred, Oprah had a big meeting with all her producers, and said, *"We're now going to be an intentional television show."* Apparently, they responded by saying, *"What is that?"* Oprah continued, *"We are only going to do shows that come from a motivation that we're going to show people the best in themselves. We are going to be a force for good, that is the bottom-line intention."*

Subject to the question you are asking yourself, you can use your answer to guide you in the moment. For instance, if your intention for the meeting you are about to run is to engage people fully, you will choose to create a listening environment, allow everyone a share of voice and build on ideas offered. If your intention as a parent is to be present for your children, you will come home at the end of a day, switch off technology and be there for them in whatever form they choose.

You can go as big or small with your questions as you like because at the end of the day your life will be a reflection of your intention.

BEING
PURPOSE-LED

Follow your passion

Having explored the distinctions between auto-pilot, choice and intention, plus the mindset shift from doing to being, the way to lead with purpose is through the quality of your being. This starts with setting a deliberate intention to be purpose-led.

Albert Einstein captured this idea when he said, *"No problem can be solved from the same level of consciousness that created it."* It is impossible to be purpose-led if you just focus on doing. We get trained to do. We get rewarded for doing. We get addicted to doing. But doing is not a solution for being purpose-led.

David was a reluctant leader. We were introduced through his HR Director; however, he was not happy to see me. He didn't believe in personal development and he didn't want to spend time with a coach. He also didn't have a lot of choice as he'd recently attended an assessment centre to inform his future and there were some consistent themes about his leadership style that needed to be addressed. Key comments included his hypercritical style that would cut people down, unrealistic pace that gave people no time to deliver quality and a tendency to be overly directive, which would crush people's freedom.

Early in our relationship I asked him about his philosophy on leadership to learn why he did what he did and what he thought about the value of his role. It was a short conversation. David's response was that he wasn't a leader, he was a technocrat (although he was already accountable for over 3,000 people), and his role was to deliver the numbers. I realized that going head on into leadership was not the answer. I suggested that we step back and explore what had shaped his career so far and to explore implications for his future. He agreed and quickly told me that his life had been uneventful and therefore it would be a short conversation. Two hours later we were still in the middle of running through David's life experience and we had to reschedule for the next day. Three more hours and David had painted a rich picture of his lifeline and the impact on his career and leadership.

There were three key values that stood out from his story – doing the right thing, setting high standards and getting the job done. These were paramount for David, strongly influenced by his father who had been a significant role model. When we looked at his purpose David was less clear. He knew that he thrived on change and challenging the status quo. He was at his best when required to achieve stretching targets. He was passionate about showing loyalty to others, including friends and family. We explored his purpose until he arrived at an end point, *"Being a creator of opportunity."* This resonated wholeheartedly and ignited his fire.

I asked David what it would be like if rather than thinking traditionally about adopting a leadership role he committed to being purpose-led? He was unsure at first because it didn't seem tangible enough. I followed up by challenging him to define what being purpose-led would look like if he was to follow being a creator of opportunity on a daily basis? He described the following:

- Seek new horizons for the company to grow;
- Encourage people to develop and succeed;
- Embrace problems as a way to learn and continuously improve;
- Build relationships to develop better outcomes;
- Stay energized to be at the top of his game;
- Leave a legacy for the company, products and people to be in a better place than when he arrived.

By connecting with the evidence of being purpose-led, David tapped into his own internal drive to be the best he could be. I then asked him to consider what would happen if these six factors became the backbone of his own leadership framework. He got it. For the first time David was able to make an authentic linkage between what was most important to him and leadership, rather than it appearing like a dry theoretical concept.

Next, we evolved his framework into a living and breathing way of leading. We created a map which gave him the clarity about what his leadership could look like:

LEADING WITH PURPOSE FRAMEWORK

	Leadership purpose indicator	What success looks like
PURPOSE **Being a creator of opportunity**	Drive company growth	Complete the targeted acquisition on time and budget
	Develop people	Ensure senior leadership team have identified natural successors by end of year
	Embrace continuous improvement	Drive a growth mindset and hold everyone accountable to implementing the change programme
	Build relationships	Provide visible leadership to strengthen key stakeholder relationships
	Stay energized	Ensure I manage my wellbeing to be on top of my game
	Leave a legacy	Create a great place to work to innovate new brands and outstanding customer service

We extended David's thinking to encompass being purpose-led in the key areas of his life. I asked David to reflect on the most significant factors for him that would indicate he was on purpose. He arrived at nurturing family fulfilment, ensuring personal wellbeing, sustaining learning and growth, investing in friendships and giving back. We then wrapped that into a personal framework:

LIVING WITH PURPOSE FRAMEWORK

	Personal purpose indicator	What success looks like
PURPOSE **Being a creator of opportunity**	Nurture family fulfilment	Enjoy great time with the family and meet everyone's needs
	Ensure personal wellbeing	Manage energy through adopting the right habits
	Sustain learning and growth	Exercise intellectual curiosity, open mindedness and passion to grow
	Invest in friendships	Spend time with compassionate friends
	Give back	Focus on meaningful causes to make a difference

David found that by putting his purpose at the heart of his work and life he was able to integrate what was most important for him and remove previous conflict about how to juggle his priorities. His decision making took on a different quality, fuelled by his purpose, enabling him to sense check his busy schedule against being purpose-led.

Being purpose-led can be a game-changer and help to establish a clear sense of direction and conviction which carries you forward. The way to do this is to take the following steps:

PURPOSE-LED STEPS

1. Know your purpose	Make sure you have clearly defined your purpose so you have absolute conviction about your reason for being.
2. Prepare your mindset	Each day, take a moment to consciously decide to put your purpose first in all situations. You may forget as you go through the day, however, at any point you can reset your intent.
3. Define what success looks like	Be clear about the evidence required to bring your purpose into fruition and to know what you want to create.
4. Take specific actions	Make a plan of the steps you will take to follow your purpose.
5. Review your outcomes	Ensure you set aside regular time to step back and reflect on your progress and challenges. This would be a good point to share your findings with a trusted confidant.
6. Encourage others to be purpose-led	As you inspire others to discover and live their purpose, it will challenge you to increase your clarity and to course correct when needed.

CHAPTER 4

A
PURPOSE
SKILLSET

COMMON SENSE TO COMMON PRACTICE

*Like learning a language, leading with purpose
is an art and a skill*

If there is an absence of being intentional to lead with purpose, then nothing will change. However, unless you master the skills to be purpose-led you will constantly fall off the rails that your purpose provides. Frustration will set in and at some point, you will probably give up on the idea of being guided by your purpose and therefore fail to sustain its value.

The good news is that there is a clearly defined set of skills that, if you put into practice, will ensure that you get better at leading with purpose one step at a time. I am a firm believer in the power of continuous improvement; in other words, focusing on incremental improvements over time, rather than expecting some big bang that will transform your life overnight.

There are six fundamental skills which if you apply as a leader, or in life, will make a significant difference to your ability to lead and live with purpose:

PURPOSE SKILLSET

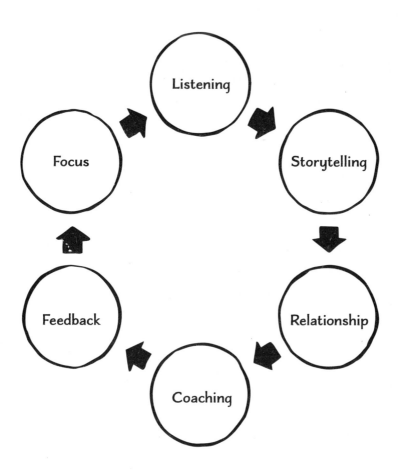

THE ART OF
LISTENING

*Poor listening is one of the biggest symptoms
of poor leadership*

What are you passionate about? This is the question I ask leaders when I get them to pair up on *'Leading with Purpose'* to develop their listening skills. They have five minutes each to learn about their partner. The results never cease to amaze me. People can discover more about each other in five minutes through genuine listening than by working alongside each other, sometimes for numerous years.

On one occasion, during a programme in America, there was a line manager and a team member on the same cohort. They chose to do this exercise together. What transpired was that the line manager learned an important nugget about his team member. Each year the team member would request a couple of days leave to take his brother to Disneyland. The manager had always granted the request but had never asked anything more. During the listening exercise, he learned that the brother was disabled and that the trip to Disneyland was the highlight of his year. Now the line manager felt humbled by the fact that he had never chosen to ask previously.

Then, I ask participants to name the qualities that make up expert listening. Responses include:

LISTENING SKILLSET

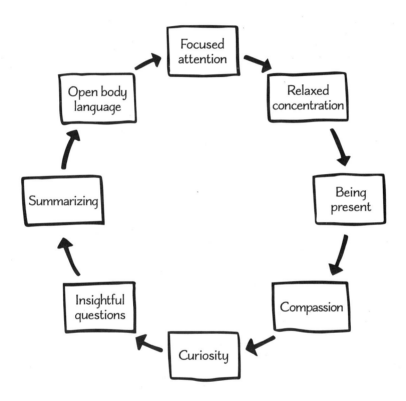

By demonstrating these qualities, you will become a great listener. This will have a profound impact on the quality of your relationships because listening puts empathy into action. It shows you care. It means people matter. It encourages you to have an open mind and stay curious. It requires you to ask questions focused on others, rather than to over-index on your own agenda. It demands that you overcome the distractions of our modern world including technology, time and transaction. Listening is a way of putting purpose into action.

In my research on listening I have identified two schools of thought:

1. The quality of content determines the quality of listening. In other words, interesting content and delivery cause great listening.

2. The quality of the listener determines the quality of delivery. Whereby through great listening it brings out the best in others.

One of the weakest leadership skills I encounter in business is listening. For instance, it makes my blood boil when I learn about capable and committed colleagues in business spending hours, if not weeks and sometimes months, preparing for internal executive presentations. Often before entering the meeting room tensions are already high because the Executive Committee is running behind and colleagues have been told to shorten their presentation. On the back foot, they enter the room, only to be greeted by bored looks, or people on their phones. As the presenters try and engage the executive they might be told to hurry up, get to the point and make their request. This is not a listening environment, and this will certainly not get the best out of others and add value to the business. In fact, it does the complete opposite. The failure to listen switches people off, sometimes to the degree that highly talented leaders want to leave the business due to poor listening skills shown.

I clearly remember as a violinist the impact of when an audience chose to listen or not. If I played to a group of children who didn't want to be there, as evidenced by the sound of whispering, rustling feet or coughing, it would be a significant distraction and thereby bring my performance down. Contrast this to when I played to a generous audience who were there for the music; then I would excel.

Everyone has the innate ability to be a great listener. However, like a muscle it needs to be exercised on a consistent basis. There are five levels of listening to be aware of:

LISTENING LEVELS

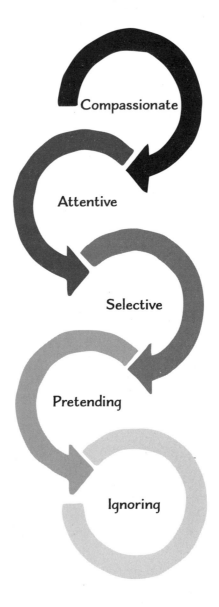

It is essential to be aware of these five levels of listening and where you spend most of your time so that you are fully cognizant about the effect you have. Do you pay zero attention? Have you become good at faking listening by nodding your head and making polite gestures, while being checked out? Do your ears stand up when the topic at hand is aligned with your agenda, only to quickly get distracted again once the moment has passed? Do you try hard to pay attention, show interest, ask relevant questions and make useful remarks?

The highest level of listening is compassionate listening. This is when you suspend your own agenda and demonstrate 100% commitment to understanding others. You are not waiting for a gap so that you can jump in with your point of view. You are not looking for the flaw in the thought process to make someone wrong. You are not questioning to catch someone out. Your genuine intent is to listen. What emerges from compassionate listening are new possibilities, alternative ideas, greater clarity, issue resolution, deeper insight and trust.

It is no surprise that one of the biggest criticisms I hear about leaders is lack of listening. Once you have a reputation for being a poor listener it's hard to shift. How well do you listen? Are you fulfilling your listening potential? What would you need to do differently to become a better listener?

Obviously listening extends beyond the workplace. However, when I ask leaders if the quality of their listening goes up or down when they are at home, guilty expressions emerge and the majority confess that when they go home their mediocre listening gets worse. Leaders tell me how they continue to check email and get distracted by work, rather than be fully present and listen with their families.

One exemplary leader I coached disciplined himself to leave his briefcase and mobile in the car so that he could walk into the house and listen to his family's state of the world, rather than stay caught up in his. Another senior executive I coached, who was head of a compliance department, had to write up a contract with her children to ensure that she listened enough to fill up their emotional account. Putting it in writing worked well to play to her conscience given her field of expertise.

At the end of the day the role of a leader is to listen. And listening, like any skill, can be improved by practising the right habits every day.

STORYTELLING
TO ENGAGE

The way to engage is through stories

Faye had just transitioned to CEO in her company. As the former chief operating officer (COO) Faye's reputation was clouded by a fear of her quick judgment on people and relentless focus on the numbers. Although these were great strengths that had helped her progress to the top, they were not necessarily going to help her succeed going forward. I was coaching her during this time and supported her in preparing for the first major offsite with her top 100 leaders. I was aware that the expectation of her initial messaging would be all about the numbers, with an underlying thought of, *"Hit the numbers and you'll be OK. Miss the numbers and you'll be out."*

Sure enough, when Faye gave me the first draft of her opening transcript it primarily focused on the delivery of the plan. I asked her about what success looked like as a result of her presentation and she said that, ultimately, she wanted to inspire and engage her team. I then challenged her to see if her current draft would fit the bill. No. We had worked together for over a year and during that time had completed the lifeline exercise to discover her purpose. She had a compelling story to tell based on the key events that had influenced her life and career, which I knew would be a great way to engage with her team and surprise them with the sharing of her humanity.

Faye agreed to develop an outline for her story. I encouraged her not to use PowerPoint, other than personal photos. When it came to her presentation she spoke from the heart. She used her photos as a way of bringing to life the points she wanted to land. The first photo showed Faye as a child working in her parents' shop, and she talked about the work ethic that she grew up with and her passion for serving customers. Her next photo brought to life her gap year travelling through Asia. One of her most poignant memories was volunteering in an Indian orphanage. This had an emotional impact on the group as she described what it was like supporting children who had nothing. Faye then shared a photo of her own children, her two sons and her daughter. One of her boys had dyed blue hair which meant Faye could talk about the importance of valuing difference and being yourself. The final picture showed Faye on the top of Mont Blanc, which was a fitting way to demonstrate her love of adventure and getting to the top.

The feedback from the team was unanimous in its appreciation about the insight that Faye had provided. Her story put together the jigsaw pieces about why she led in the way she did through revealing her core drivers of delivering brilliant service, working hard, realizing potential, embracing diversity and inclusion, and achieving high performance. From Susan's perspective, she felt on track with her purpose, *"To bring the best out of others and achieve greatness."* She recognized that through sharing her story it laid the foundations to lead with purpose and take people with her.

Stories connect. Stories build relationships. Stories provide insight. Stories are the most powerful way to communicate in a compelling way. To lead with purpose means building the skillset to create and share stories, which will bring your purpose to life. This starts with creating and sharing your personal story. Here are a couple of examples of how leaders have used their story to engage and build the necessary trust to lead others, build high performing teams and demonstrate what they stand for as a leader:

When Paul moved into the energy sector, it was a very different world to his previous role leading a department for a major FMCG company. His new organization had a strong culture based on rock solid values, however, it had been under huge amounts of political and consumer pressure and had lost its way. Paul had a clear purpose and set of values and wanted to quickly engage his team with what he stood for and to help create shared understanding in a meaningful way. We organized a team offsite with this in mind and met in a country hotel to set the right tone. As part of the pre-work the team had been asked to prepare their personal story based on three major events that had shaped their life, lessons learned and how those experiences had informed their core values. Alongside this they were asked to start reflecting on their personal purpose based on when they were at their best.

Paul opened the storytelling to set the tone. He shared personal stories to bring to life his core values which included focus, fairness and family. He had powerful personal examples to contextualize his values and one team member said that his short story had saved them six months of trying to figure him out! The team followed suit. In particular, there was one memorable moment where the longest serving member of the team, who had a tough exterior, confided a personal anecdote about the loss of one of his children at childbirth. The team was not aware of this situation and it unlocked a level of compassion for the team member not previously evidenced.

Sally had joined a professional services firm. Previously from the banking world it was a cultural shift to move from a highly directive company to one based on collaboration. One comment that was often made about Sally from her team which flawed her was a lack of trust. She prided herself on building high performing teams with trust at the centre so this was a new piece of data that she hadn't experienced before. We agreed to address the issue with a development session designed to get to the root of what was going on. I encouraged the use of storytelling to build relationship and give deeper insight about where people were coming from. This gave Sally the opportunity to disclose a level of vulnerability which the team were not expecting. It immediately broke down barriers and created the right environment to address the trust issues in a constructive way.

Here are six techniques for being a great storyteller:

1. Be clear about your purpose

Being rooted in your purpose provides a compelling reason for why you do what you do and why you are sharing what you are sharing. Lack of clarity about your purpose will create a gap in your ability to engage and inspire others.

2. Be authentic

Being yourself means having the ability to show up as your real self and to connect with others in an open and transparent way. In your storytelling, it's critical that people get who you really are.

3. **Apply the rule of three**
   I'm a great believer in sticking to the rule of three – landing three key points with any message.
   - If it's your personal story, then share three key themes linking to your purpose to illustrate your big 'why'.
   - If it's about your company vision, share three key themes to illustrate the direction you want to go.

4. **Keep your stories short**
   Have a clear beginning, middle and end. Short is compelling. Brevity equals clarity.

5. **Be creative**
   Explore your use of language, metaphors, imagery, descriptions and parables that have emotional associations to intensify your story and which bring your facts to life.

6. **Practice**
   Storytelling is an art which you can improve. Early on in my career I received a powerful piece of feedback from a leader who said that I should share my own stories in order to make my presentations more real. Then, I practised storytelling and now I receive feedback that people value my stories and want more.

Whatever your professional role, stories deepen trust. They make linkages. They develop relationships. They humanize the workplace. In communities, stories build bridges. In families, stories create connections and memories. In a world where our attention is quickly compromised, becoming a compelling storyteller is an essential skill to inspire and engage others.

COACHING2LEAD

*Coaching enables people to go beyond
what they thought was possible*

Coaching is a learning approach with its origins based in the Socratic method of eliciting truth through questions and answers. It has huge relevancy in a wide range of situations, including as a parent developing children, as a teacher educating students, as a friend supporting others and as a leader unlocking potential. Coaching is based on the premise that people have answers within them, and that through a process of inquiry to stimulate thinking and reflection, solutions will emerge. The individual in the coaching role needs to believe that others have the potential within them to arrive at their own conclusions, otherwise they will quickly revert to a directive style of communication and tell people what they think they should do. This might be well intentioned, but in the long term it will diminish the effect of people learning for themselves and developing their own ability.

What is on your mind? This was the first question I asked David on a coaching programme I was facilitating. He had volunteered to be coached in front of his peers, a group of 24 engineers. On being asked the question, David paused, put his head in his hands and stayed there for what seemed an eternity. With heavy emotion in his voice he confided that the previous year he had worked on a high-profile programme in the organization which had failed, costing several million pounds. The Director heading up the programme held him accountable. This experience had broken David's belief in his ability and dented his reputation. Up until this point he had not shared this with anyone, including his wife.

I gave David space to reflect. I asked him what outcome he would like as a result of our coaching conversation. He wanted resolution about what had happened and a way forward. We only had 30 minutes; however, by asking a series of insightful questions, he recognized that he definitely did not have sole accountability for the failed project. David then came up with a series of tangible steps to get resolution, starting with a process to collect a broad range of feedback about the project and his contribution. This would ensure that he had a robust fact base before circling back to the Director and have a direct conversation to clear the air. I know that if I had told David that he did not have sole accountability and to go and check his facts, it would not have had the same impact as arriving at his own conclusion.

The essence of coaching is to unlock potential to achieve high performance. It is based on a fundamental hypothesis:

COACHING HYPOTHESIS

PERFORMANCE

=

POTENTIAL - INTERFERENCE

Your performance is equal to potential less interference. In other words, if you are able to identify, reduce or eliminate interference, you get a closer relationship between potential and performance. This requires you to focus on root cause issues, rather than get distracted by secondary matters. It is usually the case that the actual solutions exist within the person or team being coached. The role of the coach is to help shine the light of awareness on the heart of the matter to generate possibilities.

A coaching approach involves a non-directive way of learning to enable others to arrive at their own answers. It is the most effective methodology I have encountered to raise awareness leading to new insight and action. The brain needs time to decompress. Coaching minimizes activation of the prefrontal cortex, which is the seat of logic. Many of the problems we face require us to step away from our rational way of thinking to allow fresh insight to emerge. Reflection allows the right hemisphere regions of the brain to be activated which are important for insight, and allows loose connections to form. When new insight does occur, it sets off a release of fast brain waves, known as gamma band brain waves, which signify that different brain regions are communicating with one another. Once insight has emerged we are in a different state to decide the right actions to be taken.

Sophia was one of the most driven and brightest leaders I had met. Originally a strategy consultant she had moved to work for a global organization in the insurance sector. Our executive coaching programme commenced as she picked up a new role as CMO for the company. This was a seismic shift in responsibilities and essentially meant Sophia had to lead a global function with several thousand people to engage. Up until this point Sophia had assessed her value through her ability to plan and push through on the delivery of big tasks. Now Sophia had to provide thought leadership and inspire her team to deliver initiatives. It was a painful process to endure as she was so wedded to doing tasks rather than leading.

Sophia had been on the receiving end of several coaching programmes, as well as numerous rounds of feedback in the past. She had reached a point of frustration hearing similar messages over the years that although people valued her intellect, drive and passion, they found her overly directive and verging on aggressive at times. We agreed to let Sophia bed down in her role before seeking feedback and started her programme by exploring her purpose. She was familiar with the concept of purpose; however, she hadn't yet arrived at a tangible conclusion. I challenged her over a series of sessions to keep digging deep. She arrived at some key themes including 'simplifying complexity, seeing progress and being in partnership'. I asked her to keep reflecting on what brought her most meaning and value.

Sophia's thought process continued with insight about accomplishing change no one thought she could do, inspiring others to deliver the impossible and delivering tangible change. These insights were underpinned by some core beliefs: *"There is always room to make things better, you can do anything and there are no constraints."* After further reflection, Sophia experienced a eureka moment and identified *"inspiring tangible change"* as her purpose. This was supported by three key criteria – optimism, bravery and authenticity.

Sophia was hugely energized by her purpose. It became the catalyst for her to step up as a leader. She recognized that the only way to fulfil her purpose was through engaging others, rather than trying to do everything herself. She was very grateful for the coaching process and admitted that if I had attempted to tell her about how to become a highly effective and inspiring leader, she would have rejected it. Coaching had increased her awareness through reflection and created new insight. It was then a natural step to take the necessary actions to lead her team.

Coaching requires a commitment to believe that people have answers within them. Similarly, to the speed that people interrupt others when listening (18 seconds), it's only too common when people express a problem for others to jump in with their point of view. Coaching requires you to suspend your opinion and to focus on drawing out insight. I learned coaching from the founder of business coaching in Europe, Graham Alexander, whom I co-authored the book *SuperCoaching* with. Graham recounted a story when he was training senior partners at McKinsey & Company back in the early 1970s. Following a demonstration of coaching to the group, one senior partner challenged Graham in a confronting way about why he hadn't just told the coachee what to do as it would have been faster and better. Quick as a flash, Graham shot back, *"Your role as a coach is to ask better questions. It's easy to tell somebody what you think they should do. It's much harder to draw out a great response."* Being a great coach requires you to 'pull' the answers out of others rather than 'push' for them.

The skillset of a coach in any environment falls into these three clear domains:

COACHING SKILLSET

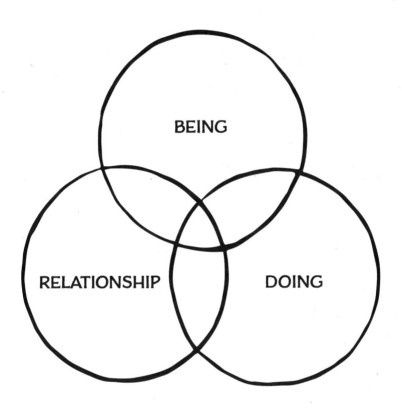

1. **Being**

   Coaching requires you to be present, be authentic and be non-judgmental to get the best out of others.

2. **Doing**

   The doing of coaching is simple. Ask insightful questions, listen to understand and summarize insight. The most popular model you can use to structure the conversation is known as the GROW model:
   - Goal – define the topic and specific outcome from the conversation;
   - Reality – explore what success looks like and identify the gap to close;
   - Options – create a variety of possibilities to resolve the issue;
   - Wrap-up – test options and agree tangible actions to progress.

3. **Relationship**

   Coaching has its roots grounded in trust, respect, support and challenge which are critical ingredients for forming a strong partnership to accelerate development.

A purpose-led leader will be fully committed to unlocking the potential of others and employing a coaching style to getting the best out of people.

FEEDBACK
CULTURES

Feedback is the art of encouragement

"I would like to give you some feedback..." What is your response to these words? Delight, or dread? Unfortunately, feedback in organizations is usually associated with underperformance, comes from above and is laced with judgment. This is the polar opposite of how it should be regarded. The true definition of feedback is that it is *'the art of encouragement'*. In giving feedback you encourage someone to keep doing what they are already doing well, or encourage them to do something differently to improve. In receiving feedback, you are inviting others to share their perspective with you about what you do well and what you could do differently to improve.

It is rare to come across organizations where feedback is a healthy exchange. At its worst, feedback is dished out twice a year in a formal and mechanistic way as a consequence of people following the performance management cycle. Even then there can be a gap in capability to give effective feedback and, as a result, I often encounter leaders who are left adrift due to the lack of valuable, insightful feedback provided.

One Friday afternoon, as I was on my way home from work, my phone rang. I was reluctant to answer; however, I saw that it was one of my senior executive coaching clients. It was unusual for Mary to call at this time. After a quick hello, she got straight to the point. *"I'm going to quit. I've had enough of my CEO."* I managed to interject and asked, *"Before you quit, what happened?"* She told me that she had presented to the main Board in the morning and had done a lot of preparation to ensure it was a success. The Board appeared enthused with her contribution and satisfied with her responses to their line of questioning. As she was leaving the office the CEO put his head around her door and mentioned that the meeting had not been her finest hour. When she requested more input all he said was that she should have been better prepared to have had more impact. He then left. The CEO gave no specific data for Mary to digest. He hadn't sought her point of view about how she thought the meeting went and, if it really hadn't met Board expectations, why hadn't they had the fortitude to share it with her in the meeting?

It was a classic case of poorly given feedback, which could have resulted in a poor outcome. I encouraged Mary to reach back out to the CEO after the weekend and request a proper review of the meeting so that if there were some pearls of wisdom to consider, then she could receive them in the right way. Monday lunchtime I got a text from Mary. She had picked up with the CEO first thing Monday morning and asked him to expand on his Friday comment. To her surprise, he couldn't even remember making the remark and reassured her that everything had gone according to plan, but if anything did arise he would inform her. It was just as well she hadn't overreacted and handed in her resignation, but there's no doubt it is a huge watch out when you give ill-timed and thoughtless feedback.

Contrast this with another CEO who had a reputation for making her one-to-ones with direct reports a highly engaging experience. Gina was passionate about the development of her people and gave considerable thought on a consistent basis about how she could help them grow and fulfil their potential. Each month she would set aside a day to focus on the team. Each member had an hour scheduled, however, it was up to them how they utilized it. Gina made it very clear that it was their time and to notify her in advance about what they wanted from the meeting. The majority of the team split the time between discussing work related issues and personal development themes. There was always one mandatory topic on the agenda – two-way feedback using a formula of 4:1. This equated to giving four examples of effective performance and one example of a personal limitation, or a blind spot. Gina was aware of research which shows how the brain needs to process four positives to one negative in order to take a balanced view. Given our natural tendency to orientate and focus on the negative, it is critical to override this wiring by highlighting what is working.

Each month Gina would collect examples of where she observed outstanding examples of performance by her team and opportunities to do things differently. She kept a file to prompt her memory and made it two-way by asking her team to do the same for her. This built a very strong feedback muscle within the team. There was a clear expectation set about giving and receiving feedback. In fact, people welcomed it so much that they often didn't wait until the monthly one-to-one. They got into the habit at the end of each weekly team meeting to review the effectiveness of the way they worked together and often found that the most productive conversation emerged in the review. They used a simple frame of 'what had worked?' and 'what should be done differently' as the method to draw out insight. The team had also agreed in their way of working to have the license to give and receive feedback in an informal way at a peer level. This meant that in day-to-day interactions feedback became integral to how they got the best out of each other.

All leaders and teams can benefit from giving and receiving regular feedback, for example, if a tennis coach gave feedback twice a year to a player, he or she would have failed long before the feedback was given at the next interval. However, in business there is still a perception that high performing executives can function at an optimum level in the absence of feedback. This is a false premise and leads to frustration, misunderstanding, poor performance and missed targets. Effective feedback can be given through three key skills; intention, emotion and data.

If your intention is to help someone learn, grow and improve, then it doesn't matter how difficult your message; the recipient will respond to the original intent. If, on the other hand, your intent is to undermine the recipient, then it doesn't matter how accurate your data is; they will respond to your intent and the data will not add value.

Feedback usually has a backdrop of emotion accompanying it. This might be a highly positive emotion like appreciation, or a negative emotion like frustration. It's important to manage your own emotion so that people get your intent, rather than the emotion. The language I encourage leaders to use is based on appreciation. For instance, saying *"Something I appreciate about your leadership is ..."* or *"Something I would appreciate you doing differently is ..."* helps to neutralize the emotion.

It's critical for feedback data to be specific, timely and focused on behaviour. For instance, if someone has an introvert personality and they receive feedback to become an extrovert, this is very unhelpful. They need to be offered specific behaviours they can adopt to achieve the intended outcome, e.g. to ask more questions in meetings so that people see them as engaged, or to have more direct eye contact to come across with more impact.

Learning to master feedback shows your commitment to helping people be the best they can be, achieving high performance and to driving learning and development.

LEADERSHIP IS
RELATIONSHIP

No relationship, no leadership

I was running *Leading with Purpose* in Singapore for IHG®. We were focused on the Asia, Middle East and Africa (AMEA) region. A General Manager (GM) attending the programme had been in charge of the InterContinental Johannesburg Sandton Towers Hotel at the time of Nelson Mandela's final year as President. There was an event at his hotel to celebrate President Mandela's achievements. Upon arriving at the hotel, the GM had the privilege of welcoming President Mandela to the hotel. Nelson Mandela had arrived slightly late, yet still took 15 minutes to greet the GM and asked a series of questions to build a relationship. The impact of this interaction had left a lifetime impression on the GM. He had been so humbled by Mandela's generosity of spirit and empathy that it had inspired the GM to go out of his way on a daily basis to connect with employees and guests to try and follow Mandela's example.

If there is one skill above all others that is required to lead with purpose it is the ability to build meaningful and enduring relationships. I would go as far as saying that leadership is relationship. Purpose-led leaders build purposeful relationships. Leaders who have no clear sense of purpose operate at a transactional level, which is a sorry comparison to being truly connected with others.

I have yet to meet anyone who has disagreed with the principle of relationships being a vital ingredient for effective leadership; however, it is rare to come across leaders who are highly skilled at building purposeful relationships. The most common scenario is that relationships get formed due to the necessity of completing a task, rather than a leader demonstrating a deep commitment to putting relationships first.

David was an exception. A master of forging strong relationships, he went out of his way to forge trusting partnerships, which formed the foundation of his leadership. As CEO of a global organization David obviously had a host of priorities to juggle, but he never forgot that relationships were his number one priority. He was a strong advocate of leadership development and would take time to attend programmes that I ran to share his leadership story and demonstrate visible leadership. David had a variety of skills he would use to build relationships.

Part of his preparation ahead of a session was to find out who was attending and to learn about recent accomplishments they had made in the company. At the start of his presentation he would go around the group, make introductions and call out a different achievement for each person. This would ensure everyone felt valued and immediately left a strong impression that if the CEO took time to find out what they had contributed, then he genuinely cared. David would then encourage everyone to ask him a question, whatever they wanted. He would make a subtle note of each question, and then over the course of his storytelling, he would weave in each person's question in a way that drew a seamless connection.

On one occasion David had joined us at the start of the day, scheduled for one hour. Ninety minutes later

David wrapped up one of the most insightful sessions I had witnessed, making a truly meaningful impact on everyone in the group. He was on his way to attend a meeting and was now running late but as he was leaving, he still paused for a few minutes to allow anyone who wanted to come and say good-bye to do so. Every act he took sent a message to people that they mattered and he cared about them.

Contrast this with another so-called leader who I had to work with who reluctantly agreed to introduce *Lead with Purpose* for a different organization. This leader had come into role post the implementation of the programme and had little interest in people and relationships. As the Chief Marketing Officer for the company, he dazzled when it came to presenting the numbers and driving promotions but demonstrated virtually zero interest in engaging others. I had to write his script word-by-word when fronting the programme to try and set him up to connect with the group, but it came across as so uncomfortable that it would have been better if he had not attended. After he had left the room I asked for feedback from the group to ascertain key learnings and insight. The group then started to share examples about this leader's behaviour back in the organization. People would actively avoid getting in the lift with him at the office as it was a painful experience to have to stand in close proximity while he glued himself to his cell phone. In meetings engagement would be solely at a level of transaction without any emotional connection made. He was virtually invisible in the office, rarely leaving his office to walk the floors and understand how people were progressing under his leadership.

The key skills for building purposeful relationships are:

1. **Define what success looks like for each relationship.** Every relationship has its own special flavour.

The clearer you are about what success looks like in the relationship, the better you will be at flexing your approach to create better outcomes.

2. **Be inclusive.** Everyone is diverse which means each person has a different way of thinking, processing information, forming beliefs, expressing feelings, demonstrating talents, living in societal contexts, preferring how they work and relate to others. It is essential to value difference in order to get the best out of every relationship.

3. **Set clear expectations.** At the heart of relationships is expectation management. Be deliberate about agreeing what you expect and don't expect in a relationship to ensure mutually agreeable outcomes.

4. **Communicate, communicate, communicate.** Become a master communicator. This means listening to understand, sharing a clear narrative, checking for understanding and agreeing solutions.

5. **Appreciate.** Who you appreciate, appreciates in value. Appreciating your relationships and making them a priority ensures that you will gain measurable value in your work and life.

It is helpful to understand the journey that relationships take so that you can map them against their various stages in order to anticipate and manage them well. What I tend to find is that people will have developed plans for strategic initiatives, projects and tasks but it is rare to come across those who have well thought through plans about how to build and nurture relationships. There are seven stages that a relationship can encounter, which enables you to navigate how they progress.

RELATIONSHIP STAGES

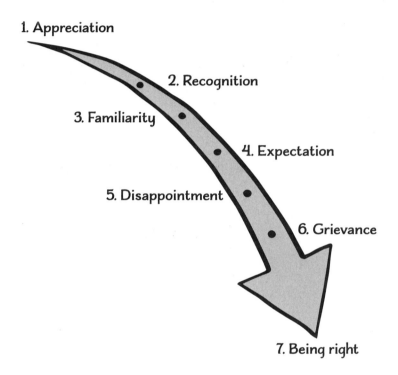

1. Appreciation

2. Recognition

3. Familiarity

4. Expectation

5. Disappointment

6. Grievance

7. Being right

In the early stages of a relationship, for instance, the arrival of a new leader, there is usually a strong sense of 'appreciation'. People 'recognize' their strengths and are filled with an optimism about what is possible. Over time, familiarity creeps in, which causes 'expectations' to be set. Usually these expectations are unspoken. The outcome of expectations is 'disappointment' as people feel let down due to expectations not being met (even if they didn't know what the expectations were in the first place!). Once disappointment has been stored 'grievance' creeps in. The final stage in the journey of a relationship is when people want to be 'right' about their point of view of others and, as a consequence, they go out to gather evidence to prove that they are right. These conversations most commonly take place around coffee vending machines or in corridors.

Although this paints a gloomy story for relationships, there is hope. The way back up to recognition and appreciation is through expectation management. It is essential to clearly agree with others about what you expect from them and what they can expect from you.

Jeremy was a high flyer in his organization. The Executive Committee believed in him and wanted to fast track his career. As a result, they decided to give him a high-profile role heading up a new division in the organization. They also gave him a new boss. Unfortunately, it was a disaster and he went from hero to zero in three months. The relationship with his boss appeared doomed. They were both highly driven people with large personalities, but had failed to clearly set expectations before Jeremy moved into role.

I received a call to mediate a conversation to try and find a solution. I started by asking both parties to define what success looked like in the relationship. They shared common ground in painting a picture where they were clearly aligned and high performing. The next step was to articulate their expectations of working together. Jeremy's boss described her desire for him to work within a tight framework where she was updated on a weekly basis. Jeremy's expectation was that he would have the freedom to approach his work in whatever way seemed fit, as long as he met his objectives and that he could update his boss monthly. They saw the gap. His boss now understood why she had felt so frustrated by Jeremy's apparent reluctance to comply in the way she had wanted. Jeremy could now see why he failed to meet the mark. They agreed a set of expectations for how to work together, which enabled them to move back up the relationship ladder and to genuinely appreciate the opportunity to work together.

There are plenty of jobs around that don't involve having to lead others. However, if you want to lead, then learn to master relationships.

FOCUS

Less is more

We live in a world of constant distraction. According to an E-mail Statistics Report commissioned by the Radicati Group, in 2015, the number of emails sent and received per day totalled over 205 billion, which equates to approximately 122 emails per person. This figure is expected to grow at an average annual rate of 3% over the next four years, reaching over 246 billion by the end of 2019.

Then add the following daily demands on leaders including the need to deliver more + faster + cheaper + better + more competition + global marketplace + less resource + constant uncertainty + security issues + M&A + 24/7.

It is no wonder we find that it's getting harder to focus on what matters most. Being anchored by your core purpose means that you are clear about what is most important and helps you navigate the modern landscape.

Simon had just transitioned to his dream role on an executive committee, a position he had been aspiring to for several years. However, as I sat down for our monthly coaching session within two weeks of him stepping up he was drowning in stuff. We started the conversation with Simon laying out every issue on his mind. I captured 43 different challenges pulling at him, noted them on post-its and stuck them on his wall. He described his current reality as 'squeezed', due to the fact that he had no time to think, he felt massive pressure to perform and drive the necessary changes that his role demanded. I asked him what success looked like and he said 'focused', which meant that he wanted to be clear about what was most important and be able to go after each requirement in a considered way. We grouped the issues into three different buckets which emerged as 1) inspiration, 2) strategy and 3) people. Simon recognized that if he didn't have the inspiration to be at his best, he would fail. If he didn't rework the strategy, the function would fail. And if he didn't get the right people in the right roles, none of it would work.

We orientated to his purpose – *"Make tangible changes to make things happen."* Simon's original background was in engineering, therefore, his core drivers were connected with understanding detail, fixing problems and moving to action. He saw that by having a broader role on the executive committee meant that he had more complexity to deal with and his past coping strategies were not going to help him succeed at the pace he wanted. We applied Simon's purpose to the three buckets and I asked him, *"What if your new role gives you bigger opportunities to make tangible changes?"* David took the first deep breath since he had transitioned up the organization. He knew that if this was the case he would be inspired. *"What if reworking the strategy helped to make things happen?"* David could see the logic and resolved to refocus on the strategy. *"What if getting the right people in the right role was the enabler to be on purpose?"* David got really fired up at this point and said that he now had the right focus to move ahead.

In his latest book *Focus*, Daniel Goleman, author of *Emotional Intelligence*, shows how our ability to focus arises from an interplay between two very different parts of the brain.

The older, lower brain, working largely outside of consciousness, constantly monitors the signals coming in from the senses. Acting as a warning system, it alerts us to things like changes in our surroundings, physical pain and memories of past anxieties. Neuroscientists call this 'bottom-up' attention, which is impulsive, uncontrolled and often triggered by fear and other raw emotions. The other part of the brain, known as the neocortex, is the brain's more recently evolved outer layer. This source of voluntary or 'top-down' attention enables us to screen out distractions and focus our mind on a single task or train of thought. Purpose is a powerful way to improve our 'top-down' wiring as we navigate the continual dance between these two parts of our brain.

As well as purpose, there are several other methods which can help to develop focus. These techniques have been developed in a variety of backgrounds and times throughout history. Each may suit the lifestyle and personal preference of a different person. These include mindfulness, exercise, nutrition, writing, thinking and conversation.

- **Mindfulness.** When I was 16, my mother took me to an introductory talk on meditation. I was fascinated to learn about how a simple, effective mental technique could allow the mind to develop a powerful state of awareness. Over 40 years later and 'mindfulness' is common practice in organizations today. In its simplest form, mindfulness means 'paying attention'. It enables you to have heightened awareness of what is going on and helps you to stop functioning on autopilot.

  To practise mindfulness, take five minutes, sit upright in a chair with your feet firmly on the floor and focus on your breath. In, out. In, out. When your mind wanders, notice where it goes (e.g. tasks, conversations, problems, noises, etc.) and then bring your attention back to your breath. Don't resist your mind's natural urge to wander, but train it to return to the present. It's best to do it close to when you wake up and just before you go to sleep; however, finding five minutes at any point during the day is a good thing.

- **Exercise.** We are familiar with the science of health and need for regular exercise. However, many people still don't build it into their everyday schedule. The key is to find what exercise works for you. Everyone has a different preference, but even the simplest guidelines from the UK NHS should be doable – 'to stay healthy, adults aged 19-64 should be active daily and do at least 150 minutes of moderate aerobic activity such as cycling, or brisk walking every week and strength exercise on two or more days a week that work all the major muscles (legs, hips, back, abdomen, chest, shoulders arms).' Exercising is a very effective way of helping you focus by increasing energy, enhancing mood, improving impulse control, boosting memory and supporting productivity.

- **Nutrition.** I was introduced to veganism in my early 20s. It was a shock to my system but I adapted well and loved the simplicity of the vegan approach. However, I missed certain food types, in particular white meat and fish. Since then I have expanded my diet and most recently teamed up with Pete Williams, an exercise and medical scientist who embraces and champions a Functional Medicine approach, to help individuals become and remain healthy. It's important to find out what food helps and prevents you from focusing clearly.

- **Writing.** Part of the joy of writing is that it cuts out all the other noise around me and enables me to put all my attention on what I'm thinking about right now. It's also a challenge because it uses a lot of concentration which is quite exhausting! One very effective writing technique is from Julia Cameron's seminal book, *The Artists Way.* As Julia explains, *"Morning Pages are three pages of longhand, stream of consciousness writing, done first thing in the morning. There is no wrong way to do Morning Pages – they are not art. They are about anything and everything that crosses your mind – and they are for your eyes only. Morning Pages provoke, clarify, comfort, cajole, prioritize and synchronize the day at hand. Do not over-think Morning Pages: just put three pages of anything on the page ... and then do three more pages tomorrow."* If you want to improve your focus about any topic write about it.

- **Thinking.** Probably one of the biggest complaints leaders have is that they have no time to think. This is a real problem because leaders are paid to think, and the quality of thinking determines the quality of outcomes. Better thinking creates better results. If you are too busy to think, you are too busy. You will have to wean yourself off the addiction to permanent busyness and make time to think. Start with five minutes a day. Where do you do your best thinking? The shower, on a walk, in the gym, on the commute? I have never heard a leader say that they do their best thinking sitting at their desk in front of a screen, or in the endless meetings they attend. How do you do your best thinking? Reflection, writing or in conversation? The best work I have come across about thinking is Nancy Kline's approach in her groundbreaking book *Time to Think*. Nancy advocates ten components to create a Thinking Environment: Attention, Equality, Ease, Appreciation, Encouragement, Feelings, Information, Diversity, Incisive Questions, Place. Applying these components will definitely increase the effectiveness of your thinking.

- **Conversation.** Research shows that leaders spend approximately 73% of their time in conversation. Conversation is a form of work and as a leader you need to develop the art of being a great conversationalist. Good conversations create focus. Bad conversations cause distraction. At the heart of conversation is compassion. You've got to be prepared to extend yourself into other people's worlds in order to create shared understanding.

Having explored the key skills for being a purpose-led leader, my recommendation is to focus on improving one skill at a time over a 90-day period. This would mean during an 18-month period you will take significant steps to becoming better at listening, storytelling, coaching, feedback, relationship building and focusing. Put that alongside discovering your purpose and shifting your mindset from doing to being and you are ready to put your purpose into action.

CHAPTER 5

PURPOSE
INTO
ACTION

THE LEADERSHIP CURRENCY

*People will forget what you said, but they
will remember how you made them feel*

I arrived in Banff, a resort town located within Banff National Park in the province of Alberta, Canada. I was there to give a keynote on leadership. Nestled within the peaks of the Rocky Mountains it was an inspiring location, suitable to challenge the top leaders of an energy company to become more inspired themselves.

I was looking forward to my talk; however, I was far more interested in learning from the other featured speaker, Bill George. Bill is a senior fellow at Harvard Business School where he has taught leadership since 2004. Prior to that, he served as chairman and CEO of Medtronic. His talk was entitled, Authentic Leadership. One of the key insights I took away that day was the following: *"Authentic leaders are constantly developing themselves to increase self-awareness and improve relationships with others. They don't hide their flaws; instead, they seek to understand them. It is a lifelong process to improve their capabilities."*

I am a big advocate of lifelong learning and I recognize that part of the human condition is having behavioural flaws which we need to manage and overcome. I have always struggled with any so-called expert who makes out that leadership is easy and there's a quick fix to lead.

When you try and distil leadership down to its essence I subscribe to the idea that authenticity is at the core. This has been validated by the fact that most leading companies globally are focusing on developing authentic leaders.

The question is how can you be authentic? The challenge to being yourself is to know yourself. You have to know yourself intimately in order to master being yourself. Think for a moment about the amount of time, energy and attention you have invested in acquiring knowledge and expertise in different fields, e.g. technical, financial, commercial, legal, sales, marketing, general business, academics, as well as your numerous personal skillsets. Then consider how much time, energy and attention you have invested in knowing yourself. I bet there is a gap!

At the core of knowing yourself is your purpose. Therefore, the act of discovering and living your purpose already puts you on a fast track for being yourself. Ken was a reluctant leader. Operating in finance he got his buzz from working the numbers and creating business solutions through his financial insight. He was a master of it and renowned in his industry. Due to his prowess, he continued to get promoted until he hit a ceiling and the next step would take him into a senior leadership role. One of the first questions I asked him in our introductory coaching conversation was about his approach to leadership. Ken admitted that he hadn't given it a lot of thought, but at this stage he believed that it would take him away from what he was best at and valued the most – working the numbers. He felt that taking a bigger leadership role would stop him from being himself. I asked him to consider what it would be like if expanding his leadership remit meant that he could become even more of himself? Ken didn't buy into the idea, but he was prepared to explore it.

We embarked on his coaching programme and started by defining his purpose and values. Overcoming his initial reluctance to the concepts, Ken quickly realized that his core value was authenticity and he articulated his purpose as, *"Keep it real."* As a result, Ken developed his leadership framework based on authenticity. We defined what success looked like for him as an authentic leader so that he had a clear measuring stick to assess his progress. Ken came up with five top measures:

1. **Delivery.** Ken was passionate about driving outstanding results and ensuring people took accountability for their performance.

2. **Talent.** Surprisingly Ken did feel strongly about attracting and developing talent so this was central to his framework.

3. **Innovation.** Ken had a creative streak and being authentic meant exploring new ideas and doing things differently.

4. **Value.** Ken was obsessed about providing value for customers, both internal and external to the business.

5. **Sustainability.** Ken knew that unless he set things up for the long term, there would be no long term. Being authentic meant truly considering all apparent trade-offs to do the right thing for all stakeholders.

With his framework in place Ken saw leadership differently. He recognized that if he was to apply these measures, he would be able to keep it real and, therefore, he would derive great satisfaction from making it possible.

Another vital component for authentic leadership is playing to strengths. What are you best at? What is the biggest difference you make? What is the real value you add?

What energizes you? A personal strength is your innate talent, what energizes you, what contributes to your growth and what makes you stronger. In 2014, research from Gallup, the American research-based global performance-management consulting company, developed a Strengths Orientation Index to help companies determine how successful they were at creating a workplace that cultivated employees' strengths. The index is made up of four items:

1. Every week, I set goals and expectations based on my strengths.

2. I can name the strengths of five people I work with.

3. In the last three months, my manager and I have had a meaningful discussion about my strengths.

4. My organization is committed to building the strengths of each associate.

Gallup tested these items using samples of the U.S. working population and discovered that 3% of employees could strongly agree with all four of the Strengths Orientation Index items. This low level of agreement shows that the vast majority of businesses in the U.S. don't focus on helping employees use their strengths. This is not local to the U.S. and it is a costly oversight. When employees feel that their company cares and encourages them to make the most of their strengths, they are more likely to respond with increased discretionary effort, a stronger work ethic, more enthusiasm and commitment.

I would go further than this and say that unless you are playing to your strengths you are not being authentic, in fact you are being a shadow of who you really are.

Hester was stepping up into a new dream role as the president of a big organization. Prior to this appointment she had led specialized functions and was concerned about the impact she would have in a broader role. As she transitioned into role I sent her the following reflection:

Play to strengths ... your ultimate value will be through what you do best ... inspiring brilliance, building strong relationships, energizing performance, leading authentically ... I believe the key is to create the right framework for people to perform and be the best they can be ... you are a master of this capability.

Hester thanked me for the reminder and increased her commitment to taking a strengths-based approach to leading authentically. One of the initial conversations she had with her new executive committee was to learn about their natural talent and agree that they would have the opportunity to leverage their strengths for the good of the organization. She asked me to facilitate their first team development offsite and we made strengths a key component of the session. Everyone completed an online strengths finder report and we used this insight to validate points of view and to utilize as a team. Not only did people find it refreshing to focus on what they were best at rather than addressing limitations, it was also a very effective way for Hester to see how to bring out the best in the team by leveraging what they did best.

Another important component for authentic leadership is to have compassion. Jeff Weiner is the CEO of LinkedIn, the prominent global business-related social networking website. Jeff played an instrumental role in LinkedIn's acquisition by Microsoft for $26 billion. He is an extremely savvy businessman, and he advocates a philosophy of compassionate leadership. In his words, *"Of all the management principles I have adopted over the years, either through direct experience or learning from others, there is one I aspire to live by more than any other. I say 'aspire' because as much as I'd like to do it consistently and without fail, given the natural ebb and flow of day-to-day operations and challenges, and the subsequent range of responses that follow, I find this particular principle harder to practise consistently than others. That principle is managing compassionately."*

Jeff describes compassion as an objective form of empathy, which is the idea of seeing things clearly through another person's perspective. This is invaluable when it comes to relating to others, particularly in difficult work scenarios. For example, when a conflict arises at work, most people tend to see things primarily through their own world view. They believe that their point of view is right and they will gather evidence to reinforce their perspective. At times, they will assume that the other person is ignorant, or has bad intentions, and they find it hard to believe that others do not agree with them.

In these circumstances, it is important to have compassion to be able to resolve conflict. What this looks like is seeking to understand why the other person has reached the conclusion they have. Jeff encourages people to ask the following questions:

- What in their background has led them to take that position?

- Do they have the appropriate experience to be making optimal decisions?

- Are they fearful of a particular outcome that may not be obvious at surface level?

Asking yourself these questions and, more importantly, asking them of others can take what could be a challenging situation and turn it into a valuable learning experience.

I was asked to coach Tony on the back of a damning performance review. Tony was a deal guy. Brilliant at driving the best deal for his company, but ruthless in his style and impact on others. It had reached a point where even though he was adding considerable financial value to the organization he was on the verge of stepping over the line of what was acceptable. It was make or break. I started our work by asking Tony to define what success looked like in his role. It was all about the numbers. He shared nothing about the way he did business, or the impact he had. After about three months working together I was struggling with his lack of willingness to re-evaluate his behaviour, as there was no change. It was coming up to Christmas and I asked Tony while on holiday to ask his two young daughters how they thought he should behave as a leader. I knew it was a risky strategy because they enjoyed the benefits of his financial drive, but I also suspected that they would encourage him to stop his aggressive behaviour.

We met up again early in the new year. I asked him what was on his mind and if he had taken the opportunity to reflect over the holiday season. Tony said that he had sought his daughters' opinion and it had caused him to stop in his tracks. They had both said independently that they felt afraid of him and unable to talk to him in the way that they would have liked. When he asked them what they would like him to do differently they simply said to listen to them without judgment or anger.

Tony had taken this feedback to heart. He looked at his anger and decided it had to stop. He could not continue in this way if it was having this level of impact at home, as well as work. The feedback from his daughters was the kick-start we needed to accelerate our work. I introduced Tony to the idea of being a compassionate leader, which he agreed with in principle. Tony was now ready for the lifeline exercise and as he revisited the formative events from his life he could clearly see the impact of his father. Tony's father had been a successful businessman, but Tony's overriding memory was of him being angry and creating an environment of fear at home. Whatever Tony achieved wasn't good enough in the eyes of his father and at some point, Tony had built a ring of steel around his heart to survive. He decided it was time to melt the steel and learn how to lead in a compassionate way. As we continued to work together to put compassion into action, I asked Tony to apply the following three steps:

1. **Seek to understand.** Tony had a habit of talking about himself while failing to show any true interest in others. I gave him the assignment to ask questions about others first to build understanding.

2. **Check for understanding.** Before responding to others Tony had to summarize in an insightful way to make sure that he had internalized the information in a genuine way.

3. **Offer to assist.** Usually it was always about Tony's agenda. One way traffic. Now he was forced to see how he could add value to others by asking them how he could help, and what they needed from him.

These three steps were painful to follow. It slowed him down in the short term, but they were critical to rebuilding his relationships and reputation in the company and to demonstrate that he could extend compassion to others. However, the main benefit was at home. Having compassion softened his stance as a father, enabled him to develop open and loving relationships with his children and learn how to be his real self.

Being an authentic leader builds trust, which is the foundation for any highly effective relationship. As you look at putting purpose into action consider the following:

PURPOSE INTO ACTION

1. How well do you know yourself in order to be yourself?

2. What specifically do you need to know more about yourself?

3. If you were truly being an authentic leader what would be different?

4. What, if anything, would stop you from being authentic?

5. What is your next step to fulfilling your potential as an authentic leader?

BOOSTING RESILIENCE

Leadership is a marathon, not a sprint

Erik Weihenmayer's accomplishments seem surreal – impossible even. He is the only blind person to climb the Seven Summits, which consists of scaling the tallest peaks on each continent. In 2014, he also solo kayaked the Grand Canyon, a journey of 277 miles along the Colorado River. Then there are his 50 solo sky dives.

In Erik's words, *"When I think about mountain climbing, I never think about conquering because if you go head to head with a mountain, the mountain will kick your butt. The mountain will destroy you. You have to have a sense of humility when you go up to climb these mountains. I've always had humility because I was, you know, having my butt kicked by blindness."*

To advance his idea, Erik co-founded not merely an organization, but rather a movement called *No Barriers*. The mission is to help people with challenges, all of us to some extent, to face barriers head on, embrace a pioneering and innovative spirit and team up with great people in order to live rich in meaning and purpose. Their motto is, *"What's within you is stronger than what's in your way."*

We experience challenges every day. One of the first books I read on personal development was *The Road Less Travelled* by M. Scott Peck. His opening paragraph went straight to my core, *"Life is difficult. This is a great truth, one of the greatest truths. It is a great truth because once we truly see this truth, we transcend it. Once we truly know that life is difficult – once we truly understand and accept it – then life is no longer difficult. Because once it is accepted, the fact that life is difficult no longer matters."*

One of the great risks in modern life is that we are sold a very different message. We are led to believe that life is easy, or should be easy, and that if it isn't then there's a problem. What if the real problem is having a lack of resilience to embrace and overcome life's challenges?

Leadership is tough. There is no doubt about it. I never cease to be amazed by the constant and relentless challenges that leaders have to face on a daily basis ... deliver turnarounds, manage organizational restructures, create sustainable business, constantly innovate, win the war for talent, satisfy stakeholders, navigate disruption, delight the customer ... the list goes on.

Resilience is the ability to recover from setbacks, adapt well to change and keep going in the face of adversity. There are three key characteristics at the core of resilience:

1. Bounceability;
2. Flexibility;
3. Stickability.

Bounceability is the idea that when faced with adversity we bounce back higher than before the situation arose as a result of our willingness to learn, grow and develop new emotional and psychological muscles. My mother sadly passed away from cancer in October 2017, following two years of painful illness. As her only son we had a close relationship which had strengthened following her divorce

34 years previously. She lived on her own and I had a great sense of responsibility to ensure she had the best possible death. As anyone who has nursed a family member through the final stages of cancer knows, it is an endurance test. My number one commitment to my mother was to honour her wish, which was to die at home. I sought to engage the NHS to find out what was possible. In July 2017, after a second period of hospitalization, mum requested that all attempts to prolong her life be stopped. At this point she was passed on to the palliative care team in the medical field. After navigating my way through the system, and with the help of her local hospice, we managed to get 24-hour care and set her up at home.

I was juggling my work, being a dad to my three children and trying to have some time with my wife. It was tough. I was exhausted. I felt bad if I wasn't being with mum, but knew I had to fulfil my work and family commitments. I spent three months on the road and had as much time as possible with mum, sleeping on a mattress next to her bed to give the care team respite. As she weakened I desperately wanted to take her out of her pain. However, I was given a clear message from her GP and hospice nurse that any form of euthanasia or assisted suicide is illegal under English law.

Thankfully, there were enough lucid moments during this time that just about made the excruciating pain she had worth it. For example, mum had unresolved issues from her marriage. So, my sister and I wrote to our father asking if he would write a letter to mum to help bring about closure to the relationship. Thankfully he sent a loving letter, which mum received with grace. She had also experienced differences in her relationship with her sister and there was still some tension. Mum was now at a point where she was unable to speak audibly. Then on one Sunday morning her sister called and out of nowhere Mum spoke clearly to say how much she loved her sister and to please let her die in peace.

When mum passed away it was a relief. We knew it was what she had wanted and overdue. She had donated her body for medical research but, unfortunately, they were not able to take it due to the impact of her cancer. We had to quickly arrange a funeral and I delivered the eulogy which enabled me to work through a lot of my thoughts and feelings. I know that as a result of the experience with mum I had grown as a person. I became stronger and clearer about life and death, and certainly have bounced back to a better state than before.

How able are you to bounce back from setbacks, adversity and disappointments? How quickly can you see a situation differently, give it a new meaning and turn an upset into a set up for opportunity?

The skill of bounceability is reframing. Cognitive reframing is a psychological technique that consists of identifying and then disputing thought patterns. Reframing is a way of viewing and experiencing events, ideas, concepts and emotions differently to find more constructive alternatives.

Jane was a high performing executive in the financial sector who had a massive drive for results. She had joined a new organization and wanted to create a fast impact; she was in a hurry to get to the top of the corporate tree. I spoke with her line manager to get feedback after ten weeks in role. He assured me that Jane had got off to a great start by building a broad range of stakeholder relationships and creating intrinsic trust through her ability to offer helpful suggestions, backed up with a willingness to be part of the solution. However, there was one relationship which could be her undoing. The previous highest performing individual in the team felt threatened by Jane's arrival. As a consequence, she was constantly sniping at Jane and testing her resilience. The dynamic came to a head at a team offsite which ironically was focused on bringing the team together. The facilitator had asked for honesty. Jane took it at face value and shared what she was having to endure in terms of backbiting and cliques. The outcome was that the colleague turned on her even more.

At our next session, I asked Jane to put herself in her colleague's shoes and to reflect on what it would be like for her having Jane come into the team. She was able to clearly see that it would be unnerving and had the potential to undermine her colleague's reputation. I asked Jane to consider what it would look like if she reframed the relationship and saw her colleague as an ally? Jane agreed in principle but was unsure about how to put this into action. A turning point happened when I challenged Jane to reach out to her colleague and to ask for guidance and counsel on business-related matters. Although this felt counter-intuitive to Jane, it unlocked the relationship because the colleague wanted to feel valued and involved. Jane's ability to reframe the relationship helped her to bounce back and rise above the previous issues being played out.

The second key characteristic of resilience is to be flexible. Flexibility is the skill of improvising through uncertainty, unknowns and unpredictability resulting in better outcomes. I see this constantly in organizations where change is the name of the game; however, most people still seek a steady state which is simply just not the case any more. For instance, the idea of having a job for life, or what has been known as 'cradle to the grave', is history. Today, the average employee stays at each of his or her jobs for an average of four years, according to the most recent available data from the American Bureau of Labour Statistics, but the expected tenure of the workforce's youngest employees is about half that.

Ninety-one per cent of Millennials (born between 1977-1997) expect to stay in a job for less than three years, according to the Future Workplace Multiple Generations @Work survey of 1,189 employees and 150 managers. That means they could have 15-20 jobs over the course of their working lives.

I was recently coaching a senior leader who had been in his organization for twenty years. During that period Adrian had covered three key functions in the organization and had a reputation as a 'safe pair of hands' through creating clear strategic plans and delivering big targets. Recently overlooked for an executive promotion, Adrian was at a pivotal time reflecting on what was right for his next career move. Rather than simply being reactive, Adrian was prepared to be flexible and embrace his career dilemma as an opportunity to shape his future for the better. We developed a career framework for Adrian to have as a lens to consider his options. The framework consisted of the following component parts:

CAREER FRAMEWORK

Personal purpose	Art of the possible
Personal values	Authenticity, honesty, fairness
Career vision	Create customer value
Personal strengths	Leadership – bring the best out of people and build high performing teams Delivery – build and deliver a robust strategic plan Commerciality – create solutions to improve key commercial drivers
Personal development	Focus – staying on track
Career options	Stay in existing organization to accelerate progression Explore new companies and different multiple roles Move into consultancy

This framework gave Adrian a foundation from which he could be flexible about his approach. He decided to accept conversations with head hunters and other organizations as a way of testing what he wanted. Previously he had shied away from engaging in any external opportunities as he had been holding on tightly to his internal position. This new level of flexibility energized Adrian. Ultimately, he stayed with his existing company, but with a refreshed way of driving his career.

How flexible are you? How effective are you at being able to improvise, see things differently and come up with multiple options to consider? One area where my flexibility gets tested is as a father! With three children, all of whom are very different, I have to flex my emotional and intellectual muscles constantly to ensure that I do not take a fixed viewpoint and come across as a rigid father. For instance, at this point the social life of my 16-year-old daughter is central to her life. Combining this with preparing for exams is a challenging mix. My 12-year-old son is transfixed by technology. Blending this with encouraging him to get out and be physically active is tough. My 8-year-old son loves to make stuff. He's never happier than when he's experimenting with a range of kitchen products to conjure up a magic recipe. Having to remind him to clear up the mess tests my patience!

The more flexible you become, the better equipped you will be as a leader. Everyone needs to be led in a different way and your ability to be flexible in your style of leadership is a fundamental requirement for success. I have identified five predominant styles of leadership which are subject to the situations leaders face:

LEADERSHIP STYLES

	Characteristic	Driver	Outcome
Visionary	Inspires belief	Think different	Direction and energy
Directive	Demands compliance	Do what I say	Crisis management
Collaborative	Builds relationships	Work together	Teamwork
Pacesetting	Drives results	Success focus	High performance
Coaching	Develops talent	Unlock potential	Succession

Most leaders have two or three preferred styles, but to be an effective leader it's important to be able to traverse across all five so that you can take people with you, give clear direction, develop win/win relationships, deliver results and unlock the potential of others.

The third characteristic needed for resilience is stickability. This is the ability to keep going in the face of adversity. When we are up against tough times it's tempting to quit, however, stickability means that we persevere, not to the extent of insanity, but certainly so that we endure what needs to be managed in order to get to the other side.

Kendra had high ambition and wanted to progress fast in her organization. Her role was about getting stuff done and she was constantly frustrated by those who didn't match her expectations and deliver at her pace. It reached the point where she was on the verge of quitting her job. During one stressful episode, when tasked with delivering a major project, we needed fortnightly coaching conversations to keep her from walking away. What made the difference for Kendra was when I challenged her to recognize that the project gave her the opportunity to accelerate her stickability and that by keeping going she would become better and stronger as a resilient leader.

What do you need to increase your stickability? I recommend the exploration of these 4 E's:

STICKABILITY

1. Energy	It's very hard to stick stuff out when you're exhausted. Managing your energy is key to keeping going.
2. Enjoyment	When times are tough, recognizing, sharing and celebrating success is vital. Success is infectious so, no matter how small an achievement, your ability to catch it and share it will be a boost for others.
3. Expertise	Sticking with situations will accelerate your learning, growth and ability to become more of a master at what you do.
4.Essentialism	This is the idea of being focused on the few vital things that make the biggest difference. Being an essentialist means saying yes to the best and discarding the rest.

SUSTAINING CONNECTIONS

We live in a relationship economy

It's simple. Great relationships lead to great results. Poor relationships lead to poor results. If you're not able to build strong and enduring relationships, your leadership will be short lived. You might get away with it in the short term as a result of power or position but, as soon as you can be ousted from your role, you will and people will celebrate. On the other hand, to lead with purpose means connecting from a position of purpose ensuring that you are genuinely linked up with others which brings a different level of meaning to a relationship.

A common pattern I see in my work is that people get promoted on technical competence and delivery. However, once they reach a certain level in an organization there is a shift. A leader requires a different skillset with the ability to connect at the heart of it. There are six key traits of a connected leader:

CONNECTED LEADERSHIP

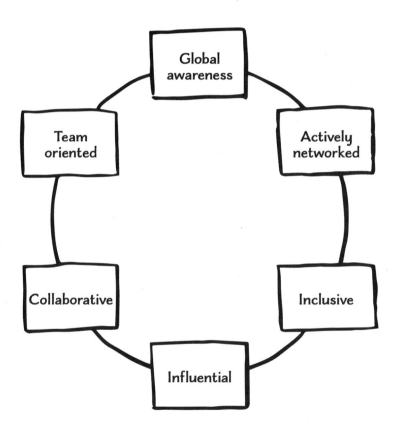

GLOBAL AWARENESS

Be aware, or be irrelevant

Patrick Cescau is the Non-Executive Chairman of IHG®. Formerly the group chief executive of Unilever Group, he was also a Senior Independent Director and Non-Executive Director of Pearson PLC, Tesco PLC, and a Director at INSEAD. In a nutshell, Patrick has very high global awareness. Several years ago, I was facilitating a leadership programme for IHG® and was fortunate to have Patrick join to discuss his key leadership lessons. One of the most profound comments he made struck a chord: *"When culture and strategy collide, culture will always win."* Or, as Peter Drucker the management guru put it, *"Culture eats strategy for breakfast."*

This is often the case in organizations when a well-defined strategic plan has been created without sufficient consideration given to the impact that different contexts, motives and understanding will have on delivering the plan. In order to succeed it is essential to create the right connections so that people are engaged, aligned and committed to act.

Carl headed up technology for a major global bank. He replaced a leader who drove silo ways of working, which had cost the company several hundred million pounds in failed projects. As a result, Carl was extremely conscious of the need to build the right culture to enable delivery of an ambitious plan. One of the first things Carl did was to bring his global leadership team together. They had never done this before due to the lack of interest from the previous leader. Carl's commitment was to help them understand each other's views about their shared plan and to agree how they were going to work together to succeed.

On the relationship side, we used personal storytelling as a way to build relationships. As people recounted what had influenced their lives, how it had shaped their values and what was most important for them, they had the opportunity to appreciate each other's cultural contexts and deep connections were formed as a team.

How would you rate your global awareness? Do you truly understand the difference between the 195 countries in the world today and the impact that it might have on your plan? You don't have to become an expert on every culture, but you do certainly need to have sufficient curiosity and compassion to ensure that you are able to build bridges to strengthen your connections.

ACTIVELY NETWORKED

Your leadership mirrors your network

Usually when I introduce the topic of being actively networked on a leadership programme it is met with high degrees of cynicism as the majority of people associate networking with manipulation, superficiality, or enduring mundane conversations over drinks. Nothing could be further from the truth. Your network defines you and you will only be as successful as the depth and breadth that your network allows. To lead with purpose means putting your purpose at the heart of your network so that it becomes a truly meaningful dimension of your world.

Paul had a big presentation coming up with his executive committee to seek approval for a major investment in his area for a telecommunications company. He had been formulating the business case for several months. His team had high expectations that Paul would do an outstanding job influencing the executive committee and securing the right investment so that they could progress with their plans. Paul spent many hours reaching out to those on the executive committee who he already felt comfortable with, sharing his plan and getting feedback. Unfortunately, he overlooked the other members who he knew less well. As soon as Paul walked into the meeting room he sensed he was doomed. The executive committee members he had not actively networked with immediately started asking difficult questions about the financial robustness of the plan and Paul felt on the back foot. Without the right level of support in the room Paul was not able to reach his desired outcome. Hugely disappointed, he admitted the error of his ways and learned a painful lesson about the need to be actively networked.

How well do you proactively manage your network? Do you leave it to chance? Are you meticulous about keeping in touch, communicating in a timely way and expanding your network? Personally, I have been challenged by the idea of networking for some of the reasons above ... it can appear like a cold, clinical sell rather than an authentic way of connecting and building relationships. As a result, I needed to give it a different meaning. I now focus on the shared value that can be created from forming networks and recognizing that through giving to others doors of mutual opportunity are opened.

Our world of social media has brought a new level of complexity to networking. At its worst, social media can drive a superficial way of networking if you approach it by simply trying to look good, but at its best social media has opened up a global network for broadening and deepening your network in purposeful ways.

DIVERSITY
& INCLUSION

Everyone has a valuable contribution to make

It is heartening to see how diversity and inclusion has become one of the most significant differentiators for organizations and leaders. A point in case has been through observing the leadership at Uber. If many of Uber's high-profile problems – the sexual harassment claims, the bullying, the intellectual property lawsuit – are attributable to former leader Travis Kalanick's brash, take-no-prisoners, admit-no-errors leadership style, then the company's new CEO Dara Khosrowshahi might be just the medicine the scandal-prone company needs. He had barely started his new role but he'd already proved his approach was the antithesis of Kalanick's. In fact, he took only seven words to do it. In a parting memo to his Expedia colleagues he wrote, *"I have to admit I am scared."* His willingness to share his vulnerability in a highly inclusive way immediately started to break down barriers and build new bridges at Uber.

Diversity is a fact. It is the mix of a wide range of factors including:

- Cognition – how we think and process information;
- Physical – who we are and what others think they see;

- Values – what we believe and how we behave;
- Societal – how we connect and relate to society;
- Occupational – what we do and how we work;
- Relational – how we relate and rejuvenate.

Inclusion is a behaviour. It is how we make the mix work and in today's global marketplace it is essential to embody both diversity and inclusion.

In a recent leadership programme I delivered on diversity and inclusion, there was a range of examples shared about how exclusion manifests in the workplace which I found disturbing. These included:

- A person refusing to attend meetings if this individual knew that a gay person would be in the room. Apparently, this individual would walk out of the meeting and openly say to strangers that they would not sit in a room with a gay person.

- A woman working in construction who on group emails would be called a 'guy'. When she questioned this terminology she then got singled out as a 'girl', rather than being called by her name.

- A man going for a promotion who was highly anxious that he would be found out as gay. He had been working in the organization for several years and had not told anyone due to the fear of how it might impact his reputation.

- An introvert who found himself constantly overlooked in meetings as a result of having a more reflective style and, therefore, not able to speak up as quickly as others.

How inclusive are you as a leader? Do not rush your answer. When you are exploring inclusive behaviour what you encounter is bias, both conscious and unconscious. Conscious bias is when you make a judgment with compelling data and information to the contrary of what you think. For instance, I have a judgment about people who say that they will complete a task by a deadline and then fail to do so. Even when I am presented with valid reasons about why they have missed the deadline, I still judge their competence. Unconscious bias is when you make a judgment without being aware that you are doing so. For example, have you ever worked with or hired someone who reminded you of another person? The feelings and opinions you associate with another person can easily influence the way you see someone else.

In my programmes I often hear claims from leaders stating that they don't have bias, until I ask them: Where is your bias (conscious and unconscious) and what impact does it have on your leadership? Responses from leaders have included:

- Dealing with different personal styles – one leader had a tendency to back off and not want to deal with people who came across as quiet or distant.

- Responding to commitment levels – one leader judged people if they didn't appear to show what he viewed as being fully committed to the organization and to doing the right thing.

- Managing gender – an IT department had very low female representation and it was recognized that even at the recruitment stage they were geared up to attract male employees, rather than an equal mix.

- Engaging suppliers – a leader recognized how they treated external suppliers as a commodity, rather than as equal colleagues.

- Welcoming different experience – a leader admitted to being dismissive of colleagues if they had less experience in tenure.

- Showing emotion – a leader judged men as 'weak' if they displayed emotion.

- Favouring graduates – an organization had a habit of looking for 'bright graduates' when they wanted a problem solved, rather than looking for a fair mix of employees.

- Promoting leaders – an organization realized that their system for promoting internal leaders was based more on tenure than competence and being fit for role.

Both conscious and unconscious bias influence how we relate to, treat, engage and position people we interact with on a daily basis. Hence, it requires high levels of awareness to overcome bias and make truly objective decisions about people and situations.

There are some key moments of choice to reinforce your commitment to being an inclusive leader:

- **Hiring.** Do you tend to recruit people in your likeness? This is a real watch out. It is critical to use recruitment to throw the net wide and challenge yourself to embrace difference before making any decisions. I have heard the argument about positive discrimination coming into play, i.e. selecting people because they are different. Everyone should be given a fair chance and your goal should be to recruit the best person for the role, regardless of your personal bias.

- **Personal development.** Development is a great opportunity to be very deliberate about developing talent so that everyone has a chance to learn and grow.

- **Performance management.** Performance management is the process of creating a work environment in which people are enabled to perform to the best of their abilities. Performance management is a whole work system that begins when a job is defined as needed and includes activities which ensure goals are consistently being met in an effective and efficient manner. This can be a highly emotive and sensitive subject where bias has to be kept firmly at bay so that performance is measured in an objective way.

- **Meetings.** It is all too common to witness meetings where the loud, extrovert members take over and the quiet, introvert members retreat. The result is that the dominant voices get heard, which is definitely not the best way to arrive at informed decision making. It is critical in meetings to actively manage this dynamic to ensure everyone has a share of voice.

- **Daily interactions.** I use an 'inclusion scale' to help leaders assess how inclusive they are being on a regular basis. I ask them to rate their behaviour using a 5-point scale:

> › 5 – High inclusion. Appreciating people and seeing their differences as strengths to leverage. Actively engaging and including them in decision making and taking them into your confidence.
> › 4 – Moderate inclusion. Accepting people for who they are and seeing their differences in a neutral way. Primarily focusing on the ways they are similar to you.
> › 3 – Average inclusion. Tolerating others however uncomfortable their differences make you feel. Treating them with respect, but doing the minimum to involve them.
> › 2 – Low inclusion. Avoiding people who are different to you. Ensuring that you don't have to work with them and deliberately excluding them.
> › 1 – Very low inclusion. An aversion to people and finding their differences unacceptable. Actively trying to remove them from the workplace and acting in aggressive and destructive ways.

It's important to be conscious of where you are on the inclusion scale and how it impacts your behaviour as a leader. We don't have to like everyone (and we won't), however, we do need to lead in an inclusive way to get the best out of everyone. Being purpose-led will help. Out of the thousands of leaders I have coached I have yet to come across anyone whose purpose causes them to judge, exclude, dismiss or discriminate against others. Each purpose can be linked to helping, enabling, inspiring, engaging, adding value, making a difference, serving and contributing to others' lives.

AGILE
LEADERSHIP

Anticipate the unknown

The new economy as shaped by artificial intelligence (AI), digitalization, automation, robotics and the gig economy is bringing levels of disruption that probably no generation has experienced at the speed we are going at today. According to the McKinsey Global Institute, at least 30% of the activities associated with the majority of occupations in the U.S. could become automated – including knowledge tasks previously thought immune. On the one hand, it is an exciting future; on the other, it brings massive uncertainty. What it will require of you as a leader is to have a deep-rooted sense of purpose, giving you a clear direction to follow, alongside a willingness to adapt and learn faster than ever before to be relevant and able to add value in whatever sector you are in.

When covering agile leadership, my programmes tend to focus on three key themes: creativity, collaboration and adaptability. I believe that these traits are at the heart of being a highly skilled agile leader, which I define as, *"The ability to anticipate and adapt to unpredictable circumstances in ways that benefit everyone."*

CREATIVITY

When faced with a problem what do you do? Seek answers from the past? Look for new data? Dig out examples of best practice? Ask for help? I have found that the research of Carol Dweck, Eaton Professor of Psychology at Stanford University, shines the light of awareness on a fundamental distinction to support creativity – the difference between having a fixed and a growth mindset. As Dweck puts it, *"Whether they are aware of it or not, all people keep a running account of what's happening to them, what it means, and what they should do. In other words, our minds are constantly monitoring and interpreting ... mindsets frame the running account that is taking place in people's heads ... the fixed mindset creates an internal monologue that is focused on judging ... people with a growth mindset are also constantly monitoring what's going on, but their internal monologue is not about judging themselves and others in this way. Certainly, they are sensitive to positive and negative information, but they are attuned to its implications for learning and constructive action."*

With automation rapidly coming down the line there is a big risk for organizations who fail to keep up. As Bob Kegan, a development psychologist who was the William and Miriam Meehan Research Professor in Adult Learning and Professional Development at Harvard Graduate School of Education, states: *"Work will increasingly be about adaptive challenges, the ones that artificial intelligence and robots will be less good at meeting. There's going to be employment for people with growth mindsets, but fixed mindsets are going to be more and more replaceable by machines. We used to say things like, 'You're going to have 6.5 jobs over the course of your career.' We should also be saying, 'You're going to have a number of qualitative shifts in your own growth and capacity over the course of your career.' This might be with the same employer, or it might be with 6.5 different employers."*

How do you nurture your growth mindset to develop your creativity? Are you relying on chance or do you deliberately challenge yourself to think differently? The growth mindset can be strengthened using three key steps:

1. **Be aware of when you adopt a fixed mindset.** This will be characterized by behaviours including: avoiding challenges, giving up easily on difficult tasks, seeing effort as wastage, ignoring useful criticism and feeling threatened by others' success. There will also be a voice in your head that, as you approach a dilemma, might tell you things like, *"Are you sure you can do this?"*, *"What if you fail?"*, *"I don't have the ability to overcome the challenge"*.

2. **Question your assumptions.** Recognize that you have a choice about how you interpret your reactions. I was coaching a team where one member received direct feedback from his peers that he was behaving as if he was half in and half out of the team. It wasn't working. Initially he assumed that the problem lay with the team's inability to accept him. However, once I challenged his assumptions he could see that he hadn't yet fully decided to be part of the team, which was impacting his behaviour.

3. **Adopt a growth mindset.** Learn to see and respond to things in creative ways. Embrace challenges. Persist in the face of setbacks. See efforts as the path of mastery. Learn from criticism. Find lessons and inspiration in the success of others. Ask for help. Show vulnerability. Be open. Think differently.

Linking creativity with a growth mindset makes it a practical way for leaders to embrace it, rather than thinking that creativity is for a select few.

COLLABORATION

In today's fast and furious world, the only way we can succeed is together. The organizations that do this best have collaborative models which proactively engage a multiplicity of stakeholders. For instance, in hospitality a company like IHG® needs to embrace colleagues, guests, owners, shareholders, suppliers, academic institutions, NGOs, government and community organizations, industry associations. In aviation, Heathrow has to meet the needs of employees, passengers, airlines, suppliers, government, regulators, communities and investors. In retail, M&S focuses on customers, employees, suppliers, investors, media, government, regulators and wider society.

Collaboration is straightforward in principle, but not easy in practice. It requires a commitment to continuously take steps to build trust, embrace difference, overcome conflict, take accountability and monitor results. My favourite principle to guide collaboration arose from a key strategic meeting I facilitated between two executive committees of a client and customer relationship. They shared a mantra, *'Better together'*; however, they failed to realize the outcome of this sentiment on a regular basis. At one point in a meeting, as they were locked in debate about potentially conflicting interests, I asked both execs to step back and define what was missing in their interaction. They had the facts. They had defined outcomes, but they stayed frustrated. At a certain point, I suggested an idea to help them work better together, *"To assume good intent, everything else is a misunderstanding."* Both parties welcomed the concept and agreed to adopt it as their guiding principle for collaboration. In future meetings, the Chair would remind both sides of the guiding principle and it would set the environment for much more productive conversations to take place.

When done right, collaboration enables agility through providing the clarity, alignment and engagement to anticipate and adapt to unpredictable circumstances in ways that benefit everyone.

ADAPTABILITY

The need for adaptability has never been greater than it is now. The ability for people, teams and organizations to adapt to different environments, stay relevant and grow is a key differentiator between success and failure. Having a clear purpose provides the platform from which we can adapt swiftly to the fast and furious demands that come our way every day. So what does an adaptable person look like? I have identified five main characteristics to embody:

1. **Adaptable people stay focused on the big picture.** In our complex world, it's essential to have a longer-term vision which pulls you in the direction you want to go, otherwise it's easy to get distracted by detail.

2. **Adaptable people experiment.** To be able to adapt you must be willing to do things differently and not get stuck in the status quo. You need to face uncertainty with a willingness to explore new ideas, rather than bury your head in the sand and hope it's going to go away. One of Google's most famous management philosophies is something called '20% time'. Founders Larry Page and Sergey Brin highlighted the idea in their 2004 IPO letter: *"We encourage our employees, in addition to their regular projects, to spend 20% of their time working on what they think will most benefit Google. This empowers them to be more creative and innovative. Many of our significant advances have happened in this manner."*

3. **Adaptable people embrace failure.** It is common to hear leaders talk about the need to fail fast in our disruptive environment. However, it is less common to see leaders put it into action. Recently I was working with

a technology team and someone in the field of big data told me how the project he was developing would be obsolete in three months! Learning from failure is how to advance quickly.

4. **Adaptable people are resourceful.** I knew one Chief Operating Officer who, in any situation, didn't just have plan B tucked up his sleeve, he also had plans C, D and E! You can take away a person's resources, but resourcefulness comes from within.

5. **Adaptable people think ahead.** They don't care about the limelight because they know it'll soon burn out. Rather than wasting effort on a temporary issue, they shift their focus to the next obstacle to get ahead of the game so that when everybody else finally jumps on board, they've already moved on to the next challenge.

We can all learn to become more agile through our ability and willingness to learn from experience and then to apply that learning to perform successfully in new situations. Ultimately, a person who is agile has more lessons, more tools, and more solutions to draw on when faced with new business and life challenges.

LEADING
CHANGE

In today's world, the fast eat the slow

Change. Whether you thrive, tolerate or resist change, there is one guarantee. Change is inevitable. The secret to making change a compelling prospect is to have a clear 'why', in other words to ensure people understand the purpose of change.

Everett Rogers, a professor of communication studies, popularized a theory in his book, *Diffusion of Innovations*, that seeks to explain how, why and at what rate new ideas spread. His research illustrated five different categories which people fall into:

DIFFUSION OF
INNOVATIONS THEORY

Category	%	Definition
Innovators	2.5	Innovators introduce new ideas, methods or products and are willing to take risks to make things happen. They are attracted to change and new experiences, and use multiple information sources for decision making. They are pioneers as leaders.
Early adopters	13.5	Early adopters tend to rely on their intuition and vision, enabling them to adapt and try new ideas, processes, products and services. They choose carefully and are influential as leaders.
Early majority	34	The early majority take a varying degree of time to adapt and respond to change. They generally wait to see whether new things are successful in practice before getting on board. They look to innovators and early adopters for positive signals.
Late majority	34	The late majority approach change with a high degree of scepticism. They are not swayed by popular messaging, but tend to rely on recommendations from friends and family to progress. They are slow to adapt.
Laggards	16	Laggards actively dislike and resist change. They tend to be focused on 'traditions', use friends and family as information sources and will only adapt to and accept change when forced to.

Stephanie loved change. The bigger the better. This fit with her core purpose which she articulated as, *"Helping make changes for the better."* She was a classic innovator, constantly generating new ideas, creating new products, flexing her organizational structure and doing things differently. However, in our coaching sessions Stephanie would often complain about the lack of pace and progress demonstrated by her team.

I conducted a feedback process about Stephanie's leadership impact with a specific focus about change and adaptability. I included a broad sweep of stakeholders, including her direct reports, peers, customers and line manager. I received an interesting picture. Stephanie's line manager and customers loved her innovation thriving on her appetite to drive change and saw it as a competitive differentiator. On the other hand, her peers and direct reports provided a different picture, citing Stephanie as bullish, egocentric and moody. They recognized her ability to create new ideas and adapt, but were disengaged by the way she went about it.

Stephanie's initial reaction to the challenging nature of the feedback was to dismiss it, claiming the comments were indicative of her peers and team's incompetence to champion change. I shared with her Everett Rogers' research to contextualize the average response to change. I also reminded her of Dr John Kotter's famous 8-Step Process for leading change:

Create a climate for change
1. Create a sense of urgency;
2. Build a guiding coalition;
3. Form a strategic vision and set of initiatives;

Engage and enable the whole organization
4. Communicate for buy-in;
5. Enable action by removing barriers;
6. Create short-term wins;

Implement and sustain change
7. Don't let up;
8. Make it stick.

Stephanie realized that because she expected others to be like her – creating and driving change – it prevented her from methodically working through Kotter's eight steps in a thoughtful way. The combination of the feedback, alongside developing a better understanding of how to lead change, enabled Stephanie to adapt her approach. The next time she wanted to bring about a change, which focused on creating a new restaurant concept, I encouraged Stephanie to bring her team together as a first step.

We gathered for a team offsite and Stephanie opened the session by talking about her purpose to help make changes for the better and how she thrived in an environment of innovation and got bored quickly with the status quo. She went on to share the insight from her feedback and disclosed her blind spot of thinking everyone was energized by change.

The team greatly appreciated her openness and asked probing questions to get a better understanding of Stephanie's expectations and how to get the best out of her, given her wiring for change. In particular, they wanted to know how they could be involved at an earlier stage in the change process to give them a chance to be fully engaged. This session addressed the first two steps of Kotter's process – creating a sense of urgency and building a guiding coalition, as the team now clearly understood why Stephanie was motivated to make change happen. The next step was to form a strategic vision and set of initiatives. The team quickly came back together with the necessary data to set them up for exploring a new restaurant concept. It is a fiercely competitive marketplace; however, they landed on an idea for a new Mexican restaurant. This was very different to anything they had tried before, having primarily delivered fast food concepts, but they were committed and agreed the necessary actions to implement the next three steps – communicating for buy-in, enabling action by removing barriers and creating short-term wins.

I asked Stephanie to reflect on the impact of her willingness to adapt and do things differently. It had been challenging for her to show vulnerability and take the risk of letting her team have greater autonomy. However, she recognized the benefits of having them engaged upfront and swiftly moving to action. Stephanie was then able to channel her efforts on not letting up and making the change stick as they had to overcome the numerous obstacles of bringing a new concept to the high street.

As a leader, it is essential to recognize that everyone is wired differently to change. I was invited to work with an executive team who had been through a series of changes, including a recent high turnover within the team itself. The purpose of the event was to accelerate the team's effectiveness in working together. We conducted a storytelling exercise where each team member shared the three main changes they had experienced in their life, the impact of those changes and lessons learned. I had been briefed by the leader that the most resistant member of the team was the engineer, who apparently was stuck in his ways as the longest serving member of the team and as the most knowledgeable from the past. This perception was quickly blown away upon hearing Rob's story. We were deeply moved when Rob shared how on the birth of his son it emerged that all was not well. His son was born handicapped with the loss of an arm. Naturally, this was a trauma for the family, but they quickly adapted and set up the right environment for his son to develop. Rob's son was fiercely competitive and loved sports. He started swimming with one arm and was determined to enter the Paralympics. This meant Rob getting up at 4am each morning to take his son swimming and working 14 hour days to raise extra funds to pay for the training.

It turned out that Rob was not resistant to change; he was simply exhausted. He had not had a break for years, working around the clock to support his family. It had reached a point where recently Rob had feared that he was on the verge of suffering a heart attack, as he had experienced considerable chest pain with the amount of pressure he was facing. This news became a turning point for the team. It was a wake-up call for the leader who realized he needed to build a closer relationship with each team member to really understand what was going on, as well as unlocking a degree of compassion within the team to have each other's back in a whole new way.

The majority of people are willing to adapt and change once they have a clear sense of purpose about why change is necessary, backed up with a strong plan to make it stick.

CAREER
SUCCESS

When your career is an expression
of your purpose you thrive

Our definition of a career needs an upgrade. It starts by developing a compelling vision that pulls you in the direction you want to go. Next, you need to integrate your core purpose and values into the heart of your career so that it becomes an extension of who you are. Your career success factors make up the non-negotiables about what you must have in place to thrive. Traditional measures include:

- Title;
- Band/level/status;
- Remuneration;
- Progression.

I encourage clients to expand their thinking and consider factors like:

CAREER SUCCESS

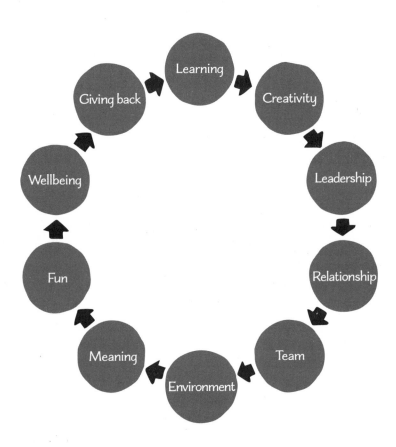

The next step is to be clear about your personal strengths to leverage and limitations to watch out for. For instance, if one of your signature strengths is to deliver at pace, then you need to be in an environment that enables you to cut through and make stuff happen, otherwise frustration will be the name of the game. Equally, if financial savviness is one of your watch outs, then make sure your role doesn't require you to spend hours on spreadsheets!

It's then helpful to develop a set of career questions to expand your mindset and probe your thinking. An example from a client included:

Who is the REAL me?
What is my leadership DESTINY?
What is the right OPPORTUNITY to be my best self?
How can I play to my STRENGTHS?
WHO do I want to spend time with?
What does this mean to my FAMILY?
What REPUTATION and PROFILE do I want to create?
What are my true RESPONSIBILITIES?
What is the impact of my FINANCIAL drive?
How do I want to GROW?

One of the outcomes from putting in this level of thought is the formation of a simple narrative, which enables you to clearly articulate your career intention with others. The final piece of the puzzle is to identify the different career options available to you and the right actions to take, such as exploring different sectors, roles, forms of business and people you can engage.

Some of my favourite sentiments about what it means to have a purpose-led career are:

"Running a business takes blood, sweat and tears, but at the end of the day, you should be building something you are proud of." Sir Richard Branson, founder of the Virgin Group

"Just because you are CEO, don't think you have landed. You must continually increase your learning, the way you think, and the way you approach the organization." Indra Nooyi, Chief Executive Officer of Pepsi Cola

"I'm here to build something for the long-term. Anything else is a distraction." Mark Zuckerberg, co-founder of Facebook

"The purpose of art is washing the dust of daily life off our souls." Pablo Picasso, artist

TOTAL
WELLBEING

At the heart of true wellbeing lies purpose

Too much to do, not enough time. Struggling to keep up. Anxiety. Exhaustion. Frustration. Burn out. Sleep deprivation. These are common states today. The idea of living in a state of harmony and wellbeing can be a forgotten memory. Waiting for the next holiday to recover is not a great strategy; for many people, as soon as they stop they get sick and just as they get better it's time to go back to work. However, it doesn't have to be the case and enjoying greater wellbeing is possible with purpose playing a central role.

Wellbeing has taken centre stage in recent years with organizations and society giving it a lot more attention. One of the main advocates of wellbeing is Martin Seligman, author of *Flourish* and the undeniable leader of the positive psychology movement. He states, *"I now think that the topic of positive psychology is wellbeing, that the gold standard for measuring wellbeing is flourishing, and that the goal of positive psychology is to increase flourishing."* His new theory of wellbeing concentrates on a set of building blocks for a flourishing life: Positive Emotion, Engagement, Relationships, Meaning and Accomplishment (PERMA). I agree with his PERMA formula; however, I believe that purpose is the consistent thread that runs through the five building blocks, without which our wellbeing will be reduced.

Joanna was suffering from a severe lack of wellbeing. A young mother with two children under five, a husband who travelled with work, a senior role in the banking sector, a weak line manager who relied on her to make the tough calls and elderly parents with cancer and dementia. It was a daunting list. We sat down in the lounge of a hotel to assess her options. I gave Joanna much needed space to download on her latest set of challenges. She was within the first six months of a new role and it wasn't playing out in the direction that she had signed up for. In particular, her line manager's 'nice' exterior was proving very difficult as it slowed down any signs of progress and made her feel on the back foot. Joanna was concerned that she was going to get labelled as the 'hatchet woman', and she described how she felt the life draining out of her.

We had been working together for the best part of a year at this stage, so I reminded Joanna of her core purpose, *"To help others be the best version of themselves."* We had also focused extensively on what living her purpose would look like at work which included:

- Being a trusted advisor giving real value;
- Every day helping the firm do things bigger and better;
- Mobilizing her team to drive change;
- Having the ability to run the function end-to-end;
- Driving the people agenda in a coaching way;
- Creating a great place to work;
- Having a strong network who are invested in her success;
- Enjoying accelerated personal and professional development.

Having this level of clarity enabled Joanna to quickly shift her focus back to being on purpose. As a consequence, we formulated a plan to share with her boss covering three key elements of how Joanna could add most value to the company, develop her team and deliver massive cost efficiencies to the business.

From a home perspective, we took another look at what being a partner, mother and daughter would mean through the lens of her purpose. Joanna could see that she was falling into the trap of being hyper self-critical and judging herself for what she believed she was not doing, rather than recognizing what she was contributing. She agreed to get some feedback from her husband to get a reality check, to work from home one day a week so that she could do the school run, and to ensure she had sufficient time to invest in her parents' care.

If we match Joanna's act of focusing on purpose against Seligman's PERMA formula we see the following:

- Positive Emotion – by taking definitive action against her purpose Joanna felt more optimistic and energized going forward.

- Engagement – Joanna reconnected with her sense of passion and commitment to making a massive difference with her company and got recharged to continue moving ahead despite the difficulties and resistance along the way.

- Relationships – the act of getting feedback from her partner, spending time with her kids and parents, alongside investing in developing her team, helped Joanna feel connected again with those who were most important in her life.

- Meaning – Joanna clearly stated that if she was going to work, while having two precious children at home, then it would really need to be meaningful, otherwise the economics didn't stack up.

- Accomplishment – her purpose fuelled Joanna to drive big changes at work ensuring that she continued to deliver her targets.

The watch out with wellbeing is that we can make it too complicated. We can be easily overwhelmed when faced with trying to integrate everything perfectly into work and life by getting enough sleep, eating right, doing regular exercise, meditating, having time to think, spending time with friends and family, reading, going on holiday, only doing the really essential things at work! The list goes on ... there is one simple tool to use to give wellbeing a chance – a wheel.

Draw a circle on a page and take the following steps:

1. What supports your wellbeing? Plot the key elements on the wheel.

2. On a scale of 1-10, mark where you are currently against each element (1 = very low wellbeing, 10 = very high wellbeing).

3. Mark where you would like to be within six months.

4. What do you believe needs to happen in order to move you in the right direction?

5. What could get in the way?

6. What steps will you take?

This will give you a simple gap analysis of where you are today, what good looks like in the future and what you believe will need to happen going forward. Once you have completed your wheel, the critical step is to stand back and ask yourself what do you think will make the biggest difference to support your wellbeing? Here's an example of my most recent wellbeing wheel:

WELLBEING WHEEL

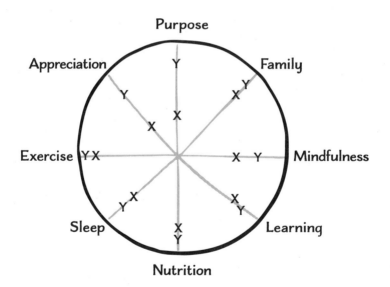

Current state = X

Future outcome = Y

When I reflected on my wheel I realized that most of the building blocks were in place. The main gaps for me were to do with purpose and appreciation. Although I am immersed in purpose, it is essential that I stay consciously connected with it through everything I do. Appreciation is another matter! I am versed with principles like 'catch people doing things right', and 'what you appreciate, appreciates in value', however, I am still conditioned to initially focus on what is not working and to spend the majority of time in the complaints department of my life! This has a real impact on my wellbeing, draining my energy. With this awareness, I was able to take tangible steps to be more purpose-led and to keep an appreciation journal, in which I would write down things I appreciated to make it a conscious act.

Getting clear about what wellbeing means to you, and focusing on the two or three vital elements that will make the biggest difference, will assist your wellbeing in multiple ways.

NURTURE
FAMILY

Family is not your purpose, however,
it can be a great expression of your purpose

When I initially ask people about their purpose many talk about family. In fact, often their responses are directly to do with family, captured in sentiments like helping their family live their best lives, fulfilling the potential of their family or helping their family be happy. I understand the power of family; however, family is not a core personal purpose and we need to learn how to blend our family with purpose in a world where divorce rates run at 42% and most people don't feel fulfilled with the amount of time, energy and effort they can dedicate to family. There are no easy answers, and everyone has to arrive at their own solution, but doing it through the lens of purpose creates a different story.

John was on track for an executive committee role for a major retailer. He had put in long hours over the last 20 years climbing up the corporate ladder and was finally knocking at the big door. There was a dilemma. With two children in their early teens, John was not sure if he was prepared to further sacrifice his family to progress his career. He knew that an executive role would require more time on the road, longer meetings and greater responsibility. I suggested that we have a joint session with his wife to explore the matter in-depth. Thankfully John's wife was very open to the idea so we set aside a good couple of hours followed by lunch.

John was already clear about his purpose, *"Making the most of life."* He was at his best when extracting the most out of every moment, which energized him and ensured that he was on track. We started the conversation by asking his wife, Carmen, to share her experience of John. She painted a mixed picture. When John was living his purpose he was open, warm, fun, engaging and the life and soul of the party. When he was off purpose he was moody, short-tempered, distracted and withdrawn. Carmen was committed to supporting John in whatever decision he made about his future, however, the critical factor for them was that he could be on purpose more of the time.

Having the mirror held up forced John to stop in his tracks. It shifted his focus from simply climbing the corporate ladder to reflecting on his family priorities. He discussed how his own father had been absent and immersed in work, and how he had followed in his footsteps. John realized that he didn't want to recreate his parents' story, but was still not sure about what actions to take.

I asked them to think about their decision making through the lens of purpose. Carmen had also identified her purpose as being passionate about nurturing others to be the best they can be. What if they were to combine their purposes to nurture others and make the most of life? This started a different kind of conversation where they were able to project into the future and challenge themselves to explore what it would be like if their marriage and family was fuelled by purpose?

I encouraged them to take some time to explore this together and to involve their children. I am a great believer in the value of scheduling family meetings, where a family sets aside about an hour each month to be able to check in and focus on important matters. The structure I recommend to conducting a family meeting is:

1. Each family member has time to express how they feel, including what they want and what support they would like from each other.

2. The family summarizes what they have heard.

3. The family member validates and makes requests for support.

4. The family offers their point of view.

5. The family member listens and takes it on board.

John and Carmen introduced this idea to their children and found it illuminating to learn more about what their two sons wanted. Both of them said how much they enjoyed having their dad around when he was in a good mood, but they also wanted him to be happy in his work.

As a result of the insight from his family, John engaged in productive conversations with his line manager to better understand the reality of the executive role. It became clear that John was on the succession plan for the executive committee but the company would not hold it against him if he decided to not progress further. I encouraged John to spend 90 days adopting the mindset of an executive committee member, which implied thinking more broadly about the whole business, rather than his immediate patch and becoming more conscious about his leadership impact. I also suggested that he dial up his commitment to making the most of life at home. As a result, John found that he had more energy, was more present and was a better person to be around. This showed him that it would be possible to progress his career, and fulfil his family wishes at the same time.

Bringing together family and purpose is a remarkable gift. It will nourish and sustain you, however great the hurdles, and it will help you to make the difficult decisions when work and family appear to get into conflict. In the final analysis, being purpose-led gives you a different lens to look through so that you can be truly fulfilled in your work, life and relationships.

IN CONCLUSION

I trust that as you come to the end of our journey together, you have arrived at a new understanding about the significance of purpose to thrive in today's world.

A personal purpose provides you with an anchor, a sense of meaning and a clear focus in a disruptive environment. A personal purpose is your reason for being. It inspires and guides your life. It is a deep conviction about what is most important that shapes your mindset, behaviour and actions.

As a reminder, seven key benefits that a purpose offers are:

1. A purpose energizes.
2. A purpose strengthens resilience.
3. A purpose helps people be at their best
4. A purpose enables creative flow.
5. A purpose ignites passion.
6. A purpose inspires.
7. A purpose connects authentically.

The vital element to the discovery of purpose is to be open-minded, curious and committed to knowing what is true for you. This is the same if you are focused on discovering a team, organizational, or even family purpose. The inquiry requires you to look at when you are at your best, in flow, fulfilled and inspired and then to align with your deepest drivers such as wanting to make a difference, add value, serve and contribute.

Living your purpose starts by setting a deliberate intention to be purpose-led in your work, life and relationships. It then requires you to demonstrate a skillset which will inspire and engage those you interact with through your ability to listen, connect and bring the best out of others.

At the end of the day life is too short to simply have a job. Leadership is not just about a position. A career is not about climbing a corporate ladder. Owning things makes life comfortable, but it's not a formula for fulfilment. Money means that you can arrive at your problems in style, but it won't buy you happiness. Fame will help you get attention, but it won't give you lasting meaning.

What if there was something that could become your guiding light, no matter how rough the elements get or how high you fly? What if you could be grounded in a state of being that would help you navigate any challenge, and enable you to keep perspective when everything is going your way? What if you had a clear framework for making big decisions and managing the big priorities in your work and life?

Having a purpose is the gateway for having an inspired and meaningful life no matter what. By discovering and following your purpose you will be on track, regardless of the obstacles you hit along the way. In fact, your purpose will give you the capacity to embrace roadblocks with a growth mindset and greater resilience. Your purpose will transform your work into a source of giving and service that will fully engage you. Your purpose will nurture your relationships so that you create new levels of communication, connection and shared reality. Your purpose will inspire you to be the best leader you can be and thereby inspire others along the way.

As a father, I am a great believer in learning from children. They have a wonderfully wise streak, which has been untouched by the world. I asked my eight-year-old son, Zebedee, about his purpose. He looked at me with his bright eyes and asked me what was a purpose. I tried to explain that it is your big 'why' in life. It is what makes you want to get up in the morning, go to school, learn and grow. He didn't quite get it so we had the following conversation:

Dad: What do you enjoy the most in life?

Zebedee: Riding my Segway hover kart (a two-wheeled, self-balancing scooter with a go-cart attached to it!).

Dad: Why?

Zebedee: Because it's fun.

Dad: How does having fun make you feel?

Zebedee: Happy.

Dad: What happens as a result of you being happy?

Zebedee: Don't know.

Dad: What's good about being happy?

Zebedee: I get excited.

Dad: What do you like about being excited?

Zebedee: It makes me feel good about life.

What if your purpose made you feel good about life? How much more would you give, share and contribute? Being on purpose becomes a virtuous circle. Be on purpose. Give. Be fulfilled. Give more. Be on purpose more.

The journey of purpose starts by clarifying your own True North and following it every day. Then you will be in a position to help others discover and live their purpose, whether it be those you lead, children you parent, or friends and family you support.

Knowing and living your purpose will bring you the clarity and resolution you seek to maximize opportunities in life. You will feel confident and passionate about the path you take and the outcomes you achieve. Once rooted in your purpose you will be lifted up to add more value, give back and help make the world a better place.

To lead with purpose is simply the greatest gift life has to offer. It lies in your hands to accept the gift and use it well.

MODELS

THE PERSONAL PURPOSE FRAMEWORK

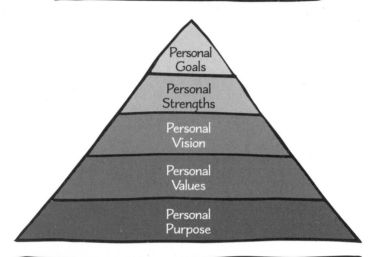

Personal Purpose	An aspirational reason for being. A deep conviction about what is most important to you. It shapes your mindset, behaviour and actions. It has a timeless quality, which is beyond circumstance. It provides the meaning and direction of your life.
Personal Values	Deeply held beliefs that drive your behaviour. Values derive from the major turning points, events and experiences that have shaped your life, which form some of your deepest learnings and conclusions.
Personal Vision	The big picture of a compelling future state. Vision lifts you up from the here and now and inspires you to move in the direction you want to go.
Personal Strengths	Natural talent and skills. Your strengths are what you are best at and enable you to be in the zone, in flow.
Personal Goals	The translation of what success looks like. Goals provide you with a clear focus and achieving them is the outcome of leading with purpose.

THE TEAM PURPOSE FRAMEWORK

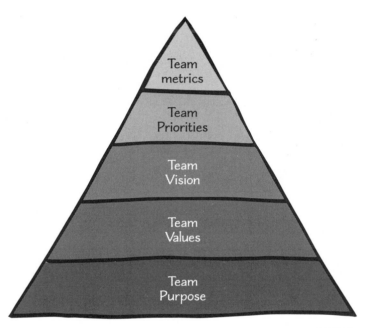

Team Purpose	Why the team exists. A clear expression of the unifying factor that brings the team together.
Team Values	How the team behaves. The shared beliefs that drive team behaviour.
Team Vision	What the team wants to achieve. The big dream that inspires and lifts up the team.
Team Priorities	What success looks like in 1-3 years. The critical strategic areas to focus on.
Team Metrics	How the team measures success. The specific targets that drive performance.

THE ORGANISATIONAL PURPOSE FRAMEWORK

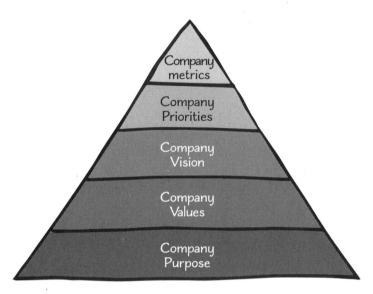

Company Purpose	Why the company exists. A clear articulation of the essence of the company and its reason for being beyond profit.
Company Values	How the company behaves. The shared beliefs that drive company culture.
Company Vision	Where the company wants to go. The ambition that inspires possibility.
Company Priorities	What success looks like in 1-3 years. The critical strategic areas that will move the company in the direction of the vision.
Company Metrics	How the company measures success. The specific targets that drive performance.

RESOURCES

The following are some of the books that have made a difference to my quest for being purpose-led:

1. *Dare to Serve: How To Drive Superior Results By Serving Others.* Cheryl Bachelder

2. *Essentialism: The Disciplined Pursuit of Less.* Greg McKeown

3. *Man's Search for Meaning.* Victor E. Frankl

4. *People with Purpose: How great leaders use purpose to build thriving organizations.* Kevin Murray

5. *Spike. What Are You Great At?* René Carayol

6. *Start With Why: How Great Leaders Inspire Everyone to Take Action.* Simon Sinek

7. *The Story of Purpose: The Path to Creating a Brighter Brand, a Greater Company, and a Lasting Legacy.* Joey Reiman

8. *Triggers: Sparking Positive Change and Making it Last.* Marshall Goldsmith

9. *True North: Discover your Authentic Leadership.* Bill George

10. *When: the Scientific Secrets of Perfect Timing.* Daniel Pink

ACKNOWLEDGMENTS

Gratitude is an expression of purpose and I am truly grateful to the following:

The team at LID Publishing who shared my purpose for the book: Martin Lui for your vision. Sara Taheri for your editorial brilliance. Shazia for your attention to detail. Matthew Renaudin for your inspired design. Miro Iliev for your website expertise. Niki, Sam and Sangeeta for your marketing skills.

The unique eye of Cambridge Jones for capturing the essence of people in your expert photography. Eg White for your creative brilliance and taking my photo.

I am deeply grateful to my clients who provide me with the opportunity to explore and deliver what it means to be purpose-led including:

Current and past leaders at IHG for championing Leading with Purpose: Andy Cosslett, Angela Brav, Christophe Laure, Craig Eister, David Cohen, Elie Maalouf, Eric Pearson, Jan Smits, Jean-Jacques Reibel, Jolyon Bulley, Heather Balsley, Keith Barr, Karin Sheppard, Kirk Kinsell, Laura Miller, Oliver Bonke, Richard Solomons, Rob Shepherd, Stephen McCall, Tracy Robbins, Will Stratton-Morris, Zareena Brown.

Current and past Chairs at the IHG Owners Association who committed to lead with purpose: Allen Fusco,

ACKNOWLEDGMENTS

Bill DeForrest, Buggsi Patel, Deepesh Kholwadwala, Kerry Ranson, Steve Ehrhardt, Tom Corcoran and to Don Berg for supporting the journey.

Julie Elder and Martin Rolfe at NATS for developing a purpose-led team.

Sian Evans at Sainsbury's Argos for your remarkable ability to get the best out of others and championing Leading with Values.

I am very appreciative of the inspirational entrepreneurs in my life who have shown how to translate purpose into great business: Andreas Thrasy, Founder and Chairman My Hotels, Grant Fuzi co-CEO & Founder Blue River Group, Renée Elliott Founder Planet Organic, Simon Woodroffe, Founder Yo! Sushi.

Thank you to my business partners who have shared common purpose: Graham Alexander, Philip Goldman and Mike Manwaring at The Alexander Partnership. Elaine Grix at Elaine Grix LTD. Avril Carson and Dr Robert Holden at The Happiness Project & Success Intelligence. Deborah Tom at Human Systems. Linley Watson at Peak Performance International.

Thank you to Brendan Barnes at London Business Forum for your enthusiasm and guidance.

Thank you to thought leaders who have inspired my work: Adam Grant, Bob Mandel, Cheryl Bachelder, Daniel Goleman, Daniel Pink, Deepak Chopra, Greg McKeown, Marianne Williamson, Marshall Goldsmith, Martin Seligman, Oprah, Seth Godin, Sondra Ray, Dr Stephen Covey, Tony Robbins, Victor Frankl.

Thank you to friends who have encouraged me along the way: Mike Mathieson, Martin Stapleton.

Thank you to my father Peter Renshaw for your purpose, passion and compassion! Thank you to my late mother Virginia Renshaw for your selfless love and support.

221

Thank you to my sister Sophie Renshaw for following your purpose.

Most importantly I am filled with gratitude for my extraordinary wife Veronica whose love, creativity and wisdom nourish me and to our amazing children India, Ziggy and Zebedee who are the ultimate expression of my purpose.

BIOGRAPHY

Ben Renshaw is one of today's foremost leadership thinkers. Speaker, coach and author of eight books, Ben's innovative work with leading organizations, senior executives and entrepreneurs has brought him international acclaim.

Formerly a classical violinist, Ben plays a different tune getting the best out of people. He believes that everyone has a purpose and that to discover and lead with purpose is the greatest opportunity in life. Ben partners with leaders and organizations focused on how to be purpose-led.

Ben's signature programmes include 'Leading with Purpose', 'Coaching2Lead', 'Leading Sustainable Growth', 'Authentic Leadership', 'Connected Leadership' and 'Agile Leadership'.

He writes about how to lead and be successful in today's volatile world with popular books: *Successful But Something Missing, SuperCoaching* and *LEAD!*

He spends time with clients like Allen & Overy, Argos, Boots, BT, Cadbury, Coca-Cola, Heathrow, Heinz, Henley Partnership, IHG®, M&S, Nationwide, NATS, NHS, P&G, Rolls Royce, Sainsbury's, SSE, Sky, UBS, Unilever, Virgin Media and Zurich.

CONTACT

For speaking and media engagements, and enquiries for Ben's leadership and corporate programmes, please contact:

Speakers Associates:
15 Kinghorn Park, Maidenhead, SL6 7TX, England
t: +44 (0) 1628 636600
e: info@speakersassociates.com
w: www.speakersassociates.com

To connect with Ben:
Twitter: @BenRenshaw
Linked-in: www.linkedin.com/in/ben-renshaw

For direct contact:
e: info@benrenshaw.com
w: www.benrenshaw.com

Sharing knowledge since 1993

- 1993 Madrid
- 2008 Mexico DF and Monterrey
- 2010 London
- 2011 New York and Buenos Aires
- 2012 Bogotá
- 2014 Shanghai